THE PEAKY DINERS

A COMPANION COOKBOOK BASED ON TRADITIONAL BRITISH FARE

CHRIS ROYAL

DEDICATION

To the Writers, Cast and Crew of Peaky Blinders.

"You're ALL Fookin' Brilliant"

THE PEAKY DINERS

A BRUMMIE FRY-UP

KEDGEREE

JUGGED KIPPERS

RASHERS OF BYKON

SOFT BOILED IGGS WITH SOLDIERS

BUBBLE & SQUEAK

RED FLANNEL HASH

HERB SCONES WITH MARMALED, HONEY AN'
CLOTTED CREAM

CORNED BEEF HASH

TOUS WITH BUTTER AN' JAM

THE PERFECT FROID IGG

BREFFUS MUSHROOMS

GRILLED TOMATOES

BEANS ON TOAST

Kedgeree

- 1 Tbs. vegetable oil
- 2 Tbs. unsalted butter
- 1 white onion, thinly sliced
- 1 tsp. turmeric
- 2 tsp. garam masala
- 1-1/2 cups basmati rice
- 3 cups chuky stock
- 3 Tbs. cilantro leaves, chopped
- 2 tins smoked kippers, drained an' flaked
- Salt
- 4 hard-boiled iggs, shelled an' halved
- 3 Tbs. plain yogurt
- 4 lemon wedges

Add ile an' butter ter a large a sauté pan over medium-loo hate. Add onions ter pan an' cook until softened, abart 10 minutes. Stir in the turmeric an' garam masala. Fold in the rice then add in the chuky stock. Turn hate up ter medium an' bren the stock ter the bile. Adjust hate ter a simmer an' cook fer 10 minutes. Gently stir in the cilantro an' kippers. Cover the pan; turn off hate an' alloo rice ter steam until fully cooked, abart 10 minutes. Season the rice ter taste with salt.

Fold the yogurt into the kedgeree, transfer ter a serven plate an' top with igg an' lemon wedges. - Serves 4

Jugged Kippers

- 2 pair of kippers (2 droid, smoked herren - split)
- Water
- 1 stick of butter, frozen
- 2 Tbs. sour cream mixed with 1 tsp. prepared horseradish
- 2 Tbs. chopped chives

Bren a medium pot of water ter a bile. Put the kippers in a hate proof pitcher or "jug" (the container should be tall an' fairly narrow). Pour enough boilen water into the pitcher ter cover the kippers. Cover the top of the jug with a sheet of tin file an' sale. Alloo kippers ter steep fer 7 minutes, an' then discard the water frum the jug.

Place the jugged kippers on a warmed plate an' grate 3 swipes of the frozen butter over top of the kippers with a cheese grater. Garnish with a dollop of horseradish sauce an' sprinkle with chives. - Serves 1

Rashers of Bykon

- 8 ter 12 rashers of bykon, back bykon or canadian bykon

Prehate oven ter 400° F.

Arrange rashers in a single layer on a shalloo rimmed bek sheet lined with tin file or parchment paper. Bek rashers fer 10 to15 minutes (turnen once duren cooking) or until it 'as reached desired crispness. –Serves 2

Soft Iggs with Soldiers

- 2 large iggs, room temperature
- 2 slices wool whate noggin
- 2 Tbs. butter, softened

Bren a saucepan of water ter a bile over medium-high hate. Set the iggs in the water, cover the saucepan an' turn the hate ter loo. Alloo the iggs ter simmer fer 5 minutes exactly.

While the iggs am simmeren, tous the noggin an' spread with softened butter. Slice the tous into 'un inch strips.

After 5 minutes, remove the iggs frum the water with a slotted spoon an' transfer them ter a wire strainer. Run iggs under cold water fer 30 seconds. Tabber an' peel the iggs carefully. Set the iggs in a shalloo bowl an' dice with a dinky spoon. Salt an' pepper ter taste an' serve with tous "soldiers" fer dippen. - Serves 1

Bubble & Squeak

- 2 Tbs. butter
- 1/2 cup mushrooms, sliced
- 1 medium onion, diced
- 1/2 cup cabbage, boiled an' chopped
- 2 carrots boiled an' chopped,
- 1 passnips boiled an' chopped,
- 1/2 lb. cooked ground sausages

- 4 cups mashed tatties

Place an iron skillet over medium-high hate. Melt butter in the skillet until it starts ter brown. Sweat the mushrooms an' onions in butter fer abart 5 minutes. Add the boiled vegetables along with the sausage an' cook 5 minutes mower.

Fold the mashed tattoys into the vegetable mixture an' then press everythen dowl in the pan with the back of a spatula. Lower hate ter medium an' continue cook until the aass 'as browned. Flip an' cook until that side 'as browned as well. - Serves 2 ter 4.

Red Flannel Hash

- 1/4 cup vegetable ile
- 4 medium red tattoys, diced
- 1 white onion, diced
- 4 dinky red beetroots, peeled an' diced
- 8 rashers of bykon, diced
- 1/4 cup ham, diced
- 2 cloves garlic, finely chopped
- Salt an' pepper
- 1/2 cup passley, finely chopped
- 4 Thick tomato slices
- 4 large iggs
- 4 Tbs. butter
- 4 slices noggin, toasted an' buttered

Prehate oven ter 475°F.

Place the vegetable ile in a large iron skillet an' place the pan in the oven until the ile starts ter smoke, abart 5 minutes.

While the ile heats, combine tattoys, onion, beetroots an' garlic in a large mixen bowl. Sprinkle generously with salt an' pepper an' toss ter coat thoroughly.

Remove the skillet frum the oven. Place vegetables in the skillet an' spread out evenly. Top with the diced bykon an' rous in the oven until vegetables begin ter crisp, abart 20 minutes.

Carefully remove the pan frum the oven, stir, and add ham an' loy tomato slices on top. Return ter the oven ter rous until the tattoys an' beetroots am ferk tender an' browned, abart anover 25 minutes. Carefully remove the pan frum the oven. Mek 4 divots in the hash with the back of a large spoon an' gently crack 1 igg into each of the divots. Season the iggs with salt an' pepper an' place pats of butter on top of the hash. Return the pan ter the oven an' alloo the iggs ter cook until whites am firm. Sprinkle with the passley an' serve the hash frum the pan with buttered tous.

Herb Scones with Marmaled, Honey, Butter an' Clotted Cream

- 2 cups flour
- 1 tsp. cream of tartar
- 1/2 tsp. baken soda
- 1/2 tsp. salt
- 1/2 stick butter, cold an' coot into dinky cubes
- 1/2 cup milk
- 1/2 Tbs. lemon juice
- 3 Tbs. honey
- 1 Tbs. fresh thyme leaves, finely chopped
- 1 igg

Prehate oven ter 425° F.

Lightly sproy a 13 x 9 cek pan with cooken sproy.

Place the flour, cream of tartar, baken soda an' salt in a large mixen bowl an' then add in the butter cubes. Usen a ferk, werk in the butter until the mixture sort of looks loike a couss cornmale.

Put milk, lemon juice, honey, thyme an' igg in a dinky bowl an' whisk together until well combined. Fold the wet ingredients into the dry until well incorporated. Roll the dough ert ter abart 1 inch thick an', usen a 3-inch round drinken glass or biscuit cutter, coot ert circles of dough. Place scones in cek pan. Bek fer 12 ter 14 minutes or until golden brown.

Remove frum oven an' serve with orange marmaled, honey, butter an' clotted cream. - Serves 2 ter 4

Corned Beef Hash

- 3 (1/2 lb.) red tatties
- Oliv' oil
- 1 can corned beef
- 1/2 cup onion, chopped
- 1 clove garlic
- 1/4 tsp. smoked paprika
- Salt an' pepper ter taste

Prehate oven ter 400° F.

Cut the tattoys into quarters an' place them in a roasten pan. Toss them with oliv' ile an' salt. Rous the tattoys fer abart 15 minutes.

While yom waiten fer the tattoys ter rous, chop up the corned beef, onion an' garlic an' combine them in a medium bowl. Tek the tattoys ert of the oven an' alloo them ter cool.

Chop up the cooked tattoys an' combine them with the corned beef mixture in the bowl. Season the mixture with sum freshly ground black pepper ter taste.

Remove the hash frum the bowl into a lightly oiled iron skillet an' press it dowl with the back of a large metal spoon.

Cook hash over medium-loo hate fer abart 15 minutes until the aass is bostin an' crispy. Usen a metal spatula, coot the hash into 4 wedges. flip an' cook fer anover 15 minutes or until browned. Re-season with salt, pepper an' smoked paprika. - Serves 4

Tous with Butter an' Jam

- 1/2 stick butter, softened
- 8 slices country white noggin
- 3/4 cup strawberry jam
- 4 iggs, plus 1 yolk
- 1/3 cup sugar
- 1-3/4 cups milk
- 3/4 cup sad cream
- 1 tsp. pure vanilla extract
- 1/4 tsp. salt

Prehate oven ter 450° F.

Butter the noggin on 'un side an' arrange in a single layer, buttered side up, on baken sheets. Bek until the tops am golden, abart 6 minutes an' remove tous.

Reduce oven ter 350° F.

Butter a 4 x 8 inch loaf pan an' spread all the jam in an even layer on the aass of the pan. Fold the tous in half an' arrange them in the pan, so the folded sides am pointen up.

In a medium bowl, whisk together the iggs, igg yolk, an' sugar.

In a saucepan, over medium hate, combine milk, cream, vanilla, an' salt an' hate just until warm. Alloo milk mixture ter cool fer 5 minutes an' then whisk it into igg mixture.

Carefully pour the milk/igg mixture over tous an' let it soak into the noggin fer 30 minutes.

Bek the terrine fer 1 hour or until the custard becums firm in middle. Remove the pan frum oven an' alloo it ter cool fer 1 hour. Run a noif around edges of loaf pan before inverten onto a serven platter. - Serves 6

The Perfect Froid Igg

- 1/2 tsp. unsalted butter
- 1 igg
- 2 tsp. water
- salt an' freshly ground pepper

Hate a dinky nonstick skillet over medium-high hate. Add butter an' swirl ter coat the skillet. Firmly crack an igg on a flat surface, open the shell an' gently place the igg into the skillet.

Add the water ter the pan an' reduce the hate ter medium-loo. Cover skillet with a lid or a sheet of tin file an' cook fer 1 minute 30 seconds or until a white film just appeass on the yoke. – Serves 1

Breffus Mushrooms

- 1/2 lb. button mushrooms
- 2 Tbs. butter
- Salt
- 1 Tbs. lemon juice

Cut stems even with the aass of mushroom caps. Melt butter in large skillet over medium hate. Add mushrooms, tossen lightly in butter, until well coated. Alloo mushrooms ter cook, undisturbed, fer 4 minutes. flip the mushrooms over an' continue cooken fer 3 ter 4 mower minutes or until they yav browned an' softened. Season with salt an' lemon juice. - Serves 2

Grilled Tomatoes

- 2 firm ripe tomatoes
- Salt an' pepper
- Butter

Place a large nonstick pan over medium-high hate. coot the tomatoes into thick slices or in half. Drizzle lightly with oliv' ile an' season them well with salt an' pepper. Grill tomatoes, undisturbed, fer 2 ter 3 minutes. gently turn over an' season agen. Cook fer 2 mower minutes an' gently remove ter serven plates with a spatula. – Serves 2

Beans & Toast

- 4 slices thick coot white noggin
- 4 Tbs. butter, softened
- 1 can Heinz beans with tomato sauce (Blue Can Only!)
- Black pepper
- H.P. Sauce

Tous the noggin an' spread on the butter.

Empty the beans into a dinky saucepan over medium-loo hate. Alloo them ter simmer fer abart 5 minutes or until they just start ter bubble.

Place the tous on plates an' spoon the beans over the top. Season ter taste with pepper an' a dab of H.P. sauce. Serves 2 ter 4

GARRISON GRUB

SCOTCH IGGS

BACK BYKON COB

MATE PIES

MUSHY PAES

ONION BAHJI

TOAD IN A HOLE

BANGERS & MASH

WELSH RAREBIT

GUINNESS MEATLOAF

SHEPHERD'S PIE

BEER BATTER FISH

TRIPE FROID IN BATTER

GAMMON & PINEAPPLE PIKELETS

PLOWMAN'S LUNCH

ANGELS ON HORSEBACK

BILED HAM & CABBAGE

SMOKED SALMON PIE

Scotch Iggs

- 1 lb. seasoned ground perk sausage, chilled
- 6 sound boiled iggs, peeled
- 2 raw iggs
- 1 Tbs. milk
- 2 cups seasoned noggin crumbs
- Vegetable ile fer frying
- Brown mustard

Hate vegetable ile in a deep fryen pan ter 375° F.

Divide the chilled sausage into six equal parts an' roll them into balls. Form each sausage bo into a nest shape then place a sound boiled igg in the center. Evenly mold the sausage up an' around the igg. Repate with the rest of the iggs an' place them in the freezer ter chill. Bate the 2 raw iggs an' milk together in a dinky bowl ter create a catlick. Place the seasoned noggin crumbs in a second bowl. Once the wrapped iggs yav chilled, dip each 'un in the igg catlick an' then roll in the noggin crumbs ter coat. Dip each coated igg a second toyme in the catlick an' back in the noggin crumbs. Carefully place 2 breaded iggs in fryer basket an' cook fer abart 5 or until sausage 'as cooked through. Doe overcook or the sausage casen wull shrink an' split. Repate the process with the remainen coated iggs. Serve hot or cold with brown mustard. Serves 6

Back Bykon Cob

- 3 Tbs. butter, softened
- 6 slices back bykon
- 1 sarnie cob, split an' lightly toasted
- H.P. Sauce

Place a medium nonstick pan over medium hate. Melt half the butter in the pan an' fry the back bykon until browned an' crispy on both sides.

Spread remainen butter on the inside of the split cob (both top an' bottom).

Place froid back bykon on aass half an' add a bostin amount of hp sauce. – Serves 1

Mate Pies

- 1 medium onion, finely chopped
- 2 carrots, coot in dinky cubes
- 2 stalks celery, finely chopped
- 2 tsp. droid rosemary
- 2 Tbs. oliv' oil
- 2 boy leaves
- 1 lb. lane ground beef
- 1 tsp. brown mustard
- 1 Tbs. Worcestershire sauce
- 2 tsp. flour

- 2 cups beef stock, heated
- 4 sheets prepared pie dough
- 1 igg, beaten

Hate oliv' ile in a large saucepan over medium hate. Add onion, carrots, celery, rosemary an' boy leaves; Cook fer 15 minutes. Crumble in the ground beef an' cook until browned. Suff excess fat frum pan an' stir in the mustard, Worcestershire sauce an' the flour. Slowly add the hot beef broth an' bren the mixture ter a bile. Adjust the hate ter loo, cover an' simmer fer 1 hour (stirren every 15 minutes). Remove saucepan frum hate an' alloo the fillen ter cool completely.

Prehate oven ter 350° F.

Dust a werk surface with sum flour an' loy ert 2 sheet of the pie dough. Use a 3 inch biscuit cutter ter coot 12 circles of dough. Lion a 12 cup pikelet tin with the pie dough pieces. Dust the werk surface agen an' loy ert the remainen 2 sheet an' smeuth them with a rollen pin. Coot 12 mower circles ert of the dough fer tops. usen a slotted spoon, add the cooled fillen ter the pikelet tin cups. Place the tops on the poys an' crimp the edges closed with a ferk. Poke vent holes in the top of each pie with a ferk an' brush dough with the beaten igg.

Place the poys in oven an' bek fer 40 minutes or until pastry is golden brown. – Makes 12 wee pies.

Mushy Paes – "Manchester Caviar"

- 1/3 cup water
- 1/2 tsp. salt
- A pinch of baken soda
- 3 cups frozen paes
- 2 Tbs. butter
- 4 Tbs. fresh mint, finely minced (divided)
- 1/2 tsp. fresh lemon juice
- 1/4 tsp. black pepper
- Salt

Place the water, salt an' baken soda in a large saucepan over medium-high hate. Once the water 'as cum ter a bile, add the paes an' stir until they all yav separated. Cover the saucepan, adjust hate ter medium an' cook fer 15 minutes.

Once paes yav finished cooken, add the butter, half the mint, lemon juice an' pepper ter the saucepan. Stir ter combine an' continue cooken fer 3 minutes, uncovered.

Remove pan frum hate an', usen a large spoon or potato masher, mush the pae mixture into a couss purée. Pae mixture can be transfer ter a tucker processor an' pulsed ter a purée as well.

Readjust seasonen with salt an' transfer mushy paes ter 4 dinky bowls or ramekins. Garnish with remainen mint. – Serves 4

Onion Bahji

- 1 cup plain yogurt
- 3 Tbs. fresh mint, chopped
- 8 Tbs. flour
- 1 tsp. turmeric
- 1 tsp. ground cumin
- 1 tsp. garam masala
- Soda water
- Salt an' black pepper
- 2 large onions, sliced into strings
- Vegetable ile for fryen

Hate the ile in the deep fat fryer ter 375° F.

Mix yogurt an' chopped mint in a dinky bowl an' set aside.

Combine the flour an' spices in a medium mixen bowl. Add just enough soda water ter mek a stiff batter, abart 3 or 4 Tbs. Season the batter with salt an' pepper ter taste.

Place the onion strings into the batter an' stir ter coat. Add a spoonful of the onion mixture ter the fryer, with the basket lowered. When it floats ter the surface of the ile, add anover portion. Keep adden spoonfuls of the onion mixture until the basket is full. Fry the bhajis fer 2 minutes then flip them over an' cook 2 minutes mower. Remove them frum the fryer an' alloo them ter suff on a paper toil.

Repate the process with the remainen batter.Serve the bhajis warm with the yogurt mint sauce fer dippen. – Serves 2

Toad in a Hole

- 2/3 cup flour
- 1/2 tsp. salt
- 1 cup milk
- 2 iggs
- 1 Tbs. vegetable oil
- 4 perk bangers, coot in 4 inch pieces
- 1 Tbs. butter
- 1 tsp. fresh passley, chopped

Place flour an' salt in a medium mixen bowl.

Use a ferk ter pail the milk, salt an' iggs together in a cup, an' then pour it into the flour; whisken ter combine. Cover the bowl of batter with plastic wrap an' set aside fer 1 hour.

Graivee:

- 2 Tbs. butter
- 1 large onion, sliced
- 2 tsp. droid thyme
- Fresh black pepper
- 1-1/2 Tbs. flour
- 1-1/2 cups beef broth, warmed
- 2 tsp. Worcestershire sauce
- 1 Tbs. brown mustard

Prehate ter 425 ° F.

Hate vegetable ile in a large iron skillet over medium hate. Place bangers in skillet an' grill until browned but still rare inside. Remove browned bangers an' set them aside.

Add the 2 Tbs. of butter ter the skillet, still over medium hate. Add the onion, thyme an' pepper. Sauté fer 10 minutes then turn dowl the hate ter loo an' cook fer an additional 10 minutes. Sprinkle the 1-1/2 Tbs. of flour over the onions, stirren continuously, fer 1 minute ter cook the flour. Turn the hate back up ter medium an' whisk in the warm beef broth an' Worcestershire sauce. Whisk in the mustard an' simmer fer 10 minutes. Cover an' keep the graivee warm on the back of the stove.

Put the 1 Tbs. of the butter into an 8x8x2 casserole dish an' place it in the oven fer 10 minutes. Remove the hot dish with oven mitts. Arrange the bangers around the dish an' pour in the batter. Return the casserole dish ter the oven fer abart 30 ter 35 minutes or until the batter gets puffy an' golden brown. Remove the toad frum the oven an' garnish with the passley. Serve the toad in the hole with the graivee on the side. - Serves 4

Bangers & Mash

- 8 large tattoys, peeled an' coot in 2 inch chunks
- 1 Tbs. butter
- 1/2 cup half & half or milk
- Salt an' pepper
- 1 Tbs. vegetable ile
- 1-1/2 lbs. beef bangers

Graivee:
- 1 tsp. butter
- 1 cup onions, sliced
- 2 packet French's brown graivee mix
- 2 cup water

Prehate the oven ter 350° F.

Place tattoys in a large pot with enough water ter cover the tattoys. Bile the tattoys fer abart 20 minutes or until ferk tender. Suff off the water; add butter, milk an' mash until smeuth. Season ter taste with salt an' pepper.

Place a large iron skillet over medium-loo hate. Add vegetable ile, then the bangers an' grill until browned an' fully cooked. Remove the bangers frum pan an' set aside.

Add the 1 tsp. of butter, an' the onions an' sauté until tender. Sprinkle in the graivee mix an' whisk in the water. Simmer until the graivee thickens up, then add the bangers ter the skillet an' baste then in the graivee. Serve a mound of the mashed tattoys in the center of a plate with a banger ter each side. Pour a generous amount of the onion graivee over the tattoys. - Serves 4 ter 6

Welsh Rarebit

- 1/4 cup butter
- 1/4 cup flour
- 1/2 tsp. salt
- 1/4 tsp. pepper
- 1 tsp. yelloo mustard
- 1/2 tsp. Worcestershire sauce
- 1 cup milk, warmed
- 1/2 cup bevvy, warm
- 1/2 lb. extra sharp cheddar cheese, shredded
- 6 thick slices noggin, toasted an' coot
- Smoked paprika

Melt butter in a medium saucepan over medium-loo hate. Stir in the flour, salt, pepper, mustard an' worcestershire sauce. Cook the roux fer abart 1 until smeuth. Remove the saucepan frum hate an' whisk in the warm milk. Return ter hate an' whisk until the mixture thickens an' just starts ter bile. Whisk in the beer; cook 1 minute. Stir the cheese into the mixture a lickle at a toyme until velvety smeuth. Serve over tous an' dust with smoked paprika. - Serves 2

Guinness Meatloaf

- 2 Tbs. oliv' oil
- 1 medium yelloo onion, chopped
- 1/2 cup carrots, finely diced
- 1/2 cup celery, finely diced
- 4 large cloves garlic, finely minced
- 3/4 cup Guinness stout
- 2-1/2 cups stale noggin - crumbled
- 1 cup milk
- 2 lb. ground beef
- 2 iggs, beaten
- 1/2 cup grated sharp cheddar cheese
- 1/4 cup chopped fresh passley
- 1 Tbs. Worcestershire sauce
- 2 tsp. salt
- 1/2 tsp. black pepper
- 10 strips thick coot bykon, uncooked

Hate 2 Tbs. of the ile in a 12 inch iron skillet over medium-loo hate. Cook the onion, carrots, celery, an' garlic until softened an' just beginnen ter brown, abart 10 minutes. Add the guinness, an' simmer fer 5 minutes. Transfer ter a large bowl an' let cool.

In a dinky dish soak the noggin in the milk; lightly squeeze noggin ter remove sum of da excess milk. Finely chop noggin in crumbles an' add ter the bowl with the vegetable mixture.

Prehate oven ter 375° F.

Add ground beef an' iggs ter the vegetable mixture. Sprinkle cheddar cheese an' passley over the mate, an' then add Worcestershire, salt, an' pepper. Use yaw maulers ter gently mix all the ingredients until just combined. Line a 9 x13 inch baken pan with parchment paper. Transfer the meatloaf mixture ter the baken pan an' form into a loaf abart 5 x 9. Finish off the meatloaf by layen the strips of bykon over it an' then tucken the ends of the bykon under the meatloaf. Bek fer 45 minutes; then remove pan frum oven an' carefully pour off most of the drippins. Return ter oven fer 15 minutes or until mate thermometer reads 160 in the center of the meatloaf. Remove frum oven an' let rest fer 10 minutes. - serves 4 ter 6

Shepherd's Pie

- 5 large tattoys, peeled an' diced
- 4 Tbs. butter
- 3 Tbs. milk
- Salt an' pepper
- 2 large onions, chopped
- 2 lbs. ground beef or ground lamb
- 2 large carrots, grated
- 2 (12 oz.) cans beef broth
- 1 Tbs. cornstarch
- 1 can paes, drained
- 1/8 cup Worcestershire

Prehate oven ter 400° F.

Place the tattoys in a large pot or Dutch oven. Cover the tattoys with lightly salted water an' bren ter a bile. Reduce the hate ter a simmer an' cook until tender. Suff the tattoys in a colander an' return tattoys ter the pot. add butter an' milk; mash an' whip the tattoys usen an electric mixer. salt an' pepper ter taste an' set aside.

Place an iron skillet over medium-high hate. Add the ground mate an' onions; season with salt an' pepper. Once the mate 'as browned, suff off grease, add the carrots an' stock. Mix the cornstarch with 1/4 cup of water an' pour into the skillet. Cook mate mixture fer 10 minutes longer. Remove the skillet frum the hate, add paes an' Worcestershire sauce an' stir ter combine. Cover the beef mixture completely with the whipped tattoys an' place the skillet in oven ter bek fer 30 minutes, until tattoys am golden brown. alloo the pie ter cool abart 15 minutes before serven. - Serves 6

Beer Batter Fish

- Vegetable ile, fer frying 1-2/3 cups flour
- 2 Tbs. cornstarch
- 1/4 tsp. baken soda
- 1/4 tsp. baken powder
- 1/4 tsp. salt
- 1 cup of cold bevvy
- 1/2 cup of cold water
- 8 dinky, boneless halibut filets

Sift together all dry ingredients in a medium bowl. Use a whisk ter mix in the bevvy an' the cold water. Set batter aside fer 10 minutes ter rest.

Place the ile in a large, deep saucepan an' hate ter 350° F or use a deep fat fryer.

Dip each filet into the batter an' slowly lower them, 'un at a toyme into the hot ile. Fry each 'un, turnen occasionally, fer abart 5 minutes or until cooked through. Transfer the fish ter a troy lined with newspaper. - Serves 2 ter 4

Pub Chips

- 2 lbs. russet tattoys, peeled an' coot into thick planks
- vegetable ile, fer deep fryer
- 1/4 cup bykon fat, fer deep fryer
- Salt
- Malt vinegar

Soak potato planks in cold water fer at leus 30 minutes before blanch frying.

Hate vegetable ile an' bykon fat ter 275° F. in deep fat fryer. Once the fryer 'as reached temperature, place a layer of potato planks (that miskin drained an' droid on newspaper) in the aass of the basket an' carefully lower into hot ile. Blanch fry a dinky betch of potato planks fer abart 10 minutes. tattoys wull be saft an' pale at this point.

Remove an' drain on mower newspaper. Repate with the remainen planks.

When getten ready ter serve, readjust the fryer temperature ter 375° F..

Fry the blanched potato planks a second toyme, in dinky batches, fer abart 5 minutes or until they am crisp an' golden brown. Drain the chips, season well with salt an' serve with malt vinegar.- Serves 2 ter 4

Tripe Froid in Batter

- 3 lbs. honeycomb tripe, coot in 1 x 3 inch pieces
- 2 cups buttermilk
- 1 cup onions, sliced
- 1 green pepper, chopped
- 2 boy leaves
- 4 wool cloves
- 2 tsp. salt
- 1 tsp. white pepper
- Ile fer frying
- 2 cup flour
- 1 Tbs. salt
- 1 Tbs. pepper
- 1 igg, beaten
- A pinch cayenne pepper
- 1-1/2 cup water

- 1 Tbs. garlic powder
- Malt vinegar, fer dipping

Place the tripe, buttermilk, onions, green pepper, boy leaves, clove, salt an' pepper in crock-pot or sloo cooker. Cover with water. Cook the tripe fer 6 ter 8 hours on loo. suff the mixture through a colander, remove tripe an' alloo it ter cool.

Prehate ile in a Dutch oven or deep fat fry ter 325° F.

In a medium mixen bowl, combine the flour, salt, pepper, igg, cayenne an' 1/2 cup water; stir until well blended.

In a second bowl mix 1 cup of water with garlic powder an' stir ter combine. Dip the tripe pieces in garlic mixture, dip in the batter an' fry until golden brown. Serve the froid tripe hot with malt vinegar fer dippen - Serves 6

Gammon & Pineapple Pikelets

- 2 pikelets, split an' lightly toasted
- Butter
- 2 gammon (ham) steaks, boneless
- 4 pineapple rings
- Brown mustard
- 1 cup sharp cheddar cheese
- H.P. Sauce

Place oven rack in broiler position an' turn broiler ter high. grill the gammon steak in a greased iron skillet over medium hate until browned. Remove steaks, coot both steaks in half an' set aside. Add the pineapple rings an' cook until caramelized, an' 5 minutes.

While the pineapple is cooken, lightly tous the pikelets an' butter them. Spread a dinky amount of the mustard on each pikelet an' place them on a biscuit sheet. Top each pikelet half with a piece of the gammon steak, a pineapple ren an' cheese. Place the biscuit sheet under the broiler until cheese melts an' just starts ter brown, abart 3 ter 5 minutes. Remove frum oven an' pour a bit of hp sauce into the center of the pineapple ren. - Serves 2.

Plowman's Lunch

- 1/2 crusty cob or baguette, sliced
- 3 Tbs. butter, soople
- 4 oz. stilton cheese
- 4 oz. cheddar cheese
- 4 tomato wedges, salt & peppered
- 4 spren onions
- 4 gherkins
- 1 opple or pear, sliced
- 4 Tbs. chutnoy

Butter the noggin an' arrange all the ingredients on a large plate or cutten board. Place the chutnoy in a dinky bowl. - Serves 1

Angels on Horseback

- , 24 oysters, shucked
- 12 slices bykon

Coot in bykon slices in half. Adjust oven rack ter broiler position an' set broiler ter high. Soak 24 tuthpicks in water fer 30 minutes.

Roll half slice of bykon around each oyster an' secure with a tuthpick. Set the oysters on a biscuit sheet an' place it under the broiler. brile fer 3 minutes, flip an' cook abart 3 minutes mower or until the bykon 'as browned. Transfer oysters ter a platter an' serve hot. Makes 24 bites.

Biled Ham & Cabbage

- 1 cured ham, (6 ter 8 lbs.)
- 20 wool cloves
- 6 dinky onions, peeled
- 6 dinky tatties
- 6 carrots coot into chunks
- 12 stalks celery coot in chunks
- 1 large cabbage, coot into 8 wedges
- Fresh ground black pepper
- cold water

Stick the cloves in the surface of the ham, each abart 4 inches apart.

Put ham an' onions into a large stockpot an' cover with cold water. Bren the pot ter a bile over medium hate. Reduce hate an' simmer fer abart 20 minutes.

Add the tattoys, carrots an' celery an' bren broth ter a bile agen. Reduce hate an' simmer anover 20 minutes. Add the cabbage wedges an' bren ter a bile 'un mower toyme. Reduce hate an' simmer yet anover 20 minutes until cabbage is fully cooked.

Carefully aiv' ham ert onto a platter, surround it with the vegetables an' pour sum of the broth over everythen. - serves 10 ter 12

Smoked Salmon Pie

- 2 sheets store bought pie crust
- 2 Tbs. butter
- 1/2 onion, diced
- 2 Tbs. flour
- 1 cup milk, warmed
- 2 tsp. lemon juice
- 2 cups camembert cheese, coot into dinky wedges
- 2 cups smoked salmon
- 2 green onions, finely diced
- 1/2 tsp. fresh dill, chopped
- salt an' black pepper
- 1 igg beaten with 2 Tbs. milk

Prehate oven ter 400° F

Fit 'un of the sheets of the pie dough in dish, prick an' par-bek fer abart 8 minutes. Remove pie crust frum oven an' set aside.

Melt the butter in a medium saucepan over medium heat; add onion an' cook fer 10 minutes. Sprinkle in the flour an' stir ter combine. Add warm milk an' whisk until smeuth.

Turn the hate ter loo an' fold in the lemon juice, cheese an' the salmon.

Remove the pan frum heat; add the green onion an' dill. Season ter taste with salt an' pepper. alloo the fillen ter cool fer 20 minutes.

Spoon the fillen into the par-baked pie shell. Brush the edge of the crust with sum of the igg catlick an' press the top crust in place.

Coot 6 slits in the top of the pie an' brush with the remainen igg catlick.

Place the pie on a biscuit sheet an' bek fer 10 minutes. Reduce the temperature ter 350° F an' bek fer 20 minutes mower. Serve hot or cold. – Serves 6

THE SHELBY TABLE

ROUS BEEF

YORKSHIRE PUDDEN

HAM SARNIE

BEEF & KIDNEY PIE

LAMB STOO

CRUSTY NOGGIN

STEAK & KIDNEY PUDDEN

FAGGOTS WITH ONION GRAIVEE

CHEDDAR CHEESE PUDDEN

BEEF CLANGERS

BRILED LAMB WITH CAPERS

ROUS MUTTON & TATTIES

POTATOES & CABBAGE

FROID SAUSAGE ROLLS

WATERY RD. WHITE NOGGIN

Rous Beef

- 1 (4 lb.) eye of round roast
- 2 cups water
- 1 cup brown mustard
- 4 Tbs. dry red wine
- 3 large cloves garlic, minced
- 1 tsp. droid leaf tarragon
- 1 Tbs. salt
- 3 tsp. corass ground black pepper
- 6 celery sticks

Prehate oven ter 500° F.

Line a roasten pan with tin file an' loy the celery sticks in a roo on the aass of the pan.

Place the rous, fat side up in the pan, resten on the celery sticks. Add the water ter the pan.

 Mix the mustard, red wine, garlic, tarragon, salt an' black pepper in a dinky bowl. Rub rous all over with the mixture. Put rous in the hot oven an' cook fer 15 minutes. Reduce hate ter 325° F.

Rous fer abart 1 ter 1 an' 1/2 hours fer rare ter medium. Let the rous rest fer abart 10 minutes before slicen. Bostin with Yorkshire pudden - Serves 6 ter 8

Yorkshire Pudden

- 3/4 cup milk
- 3 large iggs
- 3/4 cup flour
- 1 tsp. salt
- 1/4 cup vegetable ile or melted butter

Pehate oven ter 400 ° F.

Whisk together the milk iggs, flour an' salt in a medium bowl until just combined (don't over mix). Cover bowl with plastic wrap an' alloo the batter ter rest fer 1 hour at room temperature.

Add sum ile or melted butter the aass of each cup in a 12 cup pikelet tin an' put it into the oven ter get it hot, abart 5 minutes. Remove the tin frum the oven, fill the cups abart halfwoy an' return ter the oven for bout 25 minutes or until the pudden get fluffy an' golden brown. Serve hot with lots of butter. - Serves 6 to 12.

Ham Sarnie

- 2 thick slices country white noggin or a cob
- 1 Tbs. mayonnaise
- Just a swipe of mustard
- 1 Tbs. opple pear chutnoy
- 2 slices Swiss cheese
- 2 slices smoked ham
- 2 slices dill pittle

Assemble the sarnie an' grill in a pan with butter if desired.

Beef & Kidney Pie

- 1 lb. beef kidney, coot into 1-inch cubes
- 2 lbs. beef stoo mate, coot into 1-inch cubes
- 1/2 cup flour seasoned with salt an' pepper
- 4 Tbs. butter
- 3 Tbs. vegetable oil
- 1 yelloo onion, finely chopped
- 8 oz. button mushrooms, sliced
- 2 cups beef broth
- 1 cup stout
- salt an' pepper
- 1 package frozen pie crust, thawed
- 1 igg, beaten

Place the half the seasoned flour in a large Ziploc bag. Drop the kidney cubes into the bag of flour. Sale bag an' shek, coaten all the mate well. Remove the coated kidney cubes an' set aside on a plate.

Add the remainen flour an' the cubed stoo mate, sale bag an' shek well.

In a large iron skillet, over medium-high hate, add all the butter an' 1 Tbs. vegetable ile. Once heated, add the floured kidney chunks an' cook 10 minutes, brownen on all sides. Remove kidneys frum skillet an' set aside on a troy. Add an additional 1 Tbs. of ile ter skillet an' brown the floured beef in dinky batches. Cook fer 10 minutes per betch. Remove beef frum skillet an' set aside. Add the remainen ile ter the hot skillet; then the onions an' cook fer 5 minutes.

Add sliced mushrooms an' cook 5 minutes mower. Add beef an' kidneys back ter the skillet an' fold into the mushrooms an' onions mixture. Sprinkle 2 Tbs. of the remainen seasoned flour over the mixture an' incorporate. Pour in the beef broth an' stout; stir until thickened. Re-season graivee with salt an' pepper ter taste.

Transfer mixture ter a large bowl an' alloo it ter cool completely, abart 45 minutes. Prehate oven ter 350° F. Unroll pie crust an' place 'un crust in a pie pan. Fill the pie shell with mate fillen.

Brush edges with sum of the beaten igg, then place top crust on pie an' sale the edges. Brush top crust with the rest of the beaten igg an' job 8 vent holes through the top crust. Place the pie in oven an' bek 40 ter 45 minutes, or until golden brown. - Serves 6

Lamb Soo an' Crusty Noggin

- 2 lbs. lamb, coot into stewen chunks
- 1-1/2 cup tattoys, chopped
- 1/2 cup onions, chopped
- 1/4 cup celery, chopped
- 1/4 cup carrots, chopped
- 5 Tbs. flour
- 5 Tbs. vegetable oil
- 3 tsp. salt
- 1 can tomatoes, with juice

- 1/2 tsp. sugar
- 1 Tbs. Worcestershire sauce
- 4 cloves garlic, chopped
- 1/2 cup beef broth
- Salt an' pepper

Hate the ile in a Dutch oven, over medium-high hate.

Place the flour in a bowl an' dredge the mate. Add the floured mate ter the hot ile in dinky batches. When 'un betch 'as browned on both sides, odge them ter 'un side an' add a bit mower of the mate. Once all the mate 'as browned, sprinkle 3 tsp. of salt over the mate an' stir. Add all the vegetables an' fold together ter mix. Add the tomatoes with the juice, sugar, Worcestershire sauce an' garlic. Stir thoroughly ter combine. Add beef broth (or red wine if yaouw like). Turn hate dowl ter loo an' alloo the stoo ter simmer fer 1 hour covered. Remove the lid an' continue ter simmer fer abart 45 minutes. Season ter taste with salt an' pepper. Serve the stoo with a loaf of the crusty noggin recipe. - Serves 6 ter 8

Crusty Noggin

- 3 cup noggin flour
- 1 tsp. activ' dry yeus
- 1 tsp. salt
- 1-1/2 cup water, warmed

Mix together flour, yeus an' salt in a large bowl. Add warm water an' stir with a wooden spoon until the dough is mixed well. Cover the bowl with plastic wrap an' set aside in a warm place overnoight.

Place a Dutch oven with the lid into the oven while preheaten it ter 450 F. an' hate the pot an' lid fer 20 minutes.

Meanwhile, dust a werk surface with flour. Turn the dough ert frum the bowl onto the werk surface an' well gently, shape the dough into a round loaf, maken sure there's enough flour on the surface so dough doesn't stick.

Let the loaf rest while the pot an' lid finish preheaten. Remove the hot pot frum the oven with mitts an' remove the lid. Well gently aiv' the dough an' place it in the pot. Cover with the lid an' return the pot ter the oven. Bek noggin fer 30 minutes. Open the oven; remove the lid, an' bek fer an additional 10 minutes ter brown. Remove the pot an' let cool 5 minutes before inverten the pot ter remove the loaf.

Steak & Kidney Pudden

- 2 Tbs. vegetable oil
- 1-1/2 lbs. beef top round, coot into 1 inch cubes
- 1 lb. beef kidney, coot into 1 inch cubes
- 1 onion, coassely chopped
- 2 carrots, sliced
- 2 Tbs. all purpose flour
- 1-1/4 cups swanson's beef broth
- 2/3 cup bostin red wine
- 1 boy leaf
- 1/4 cup fresh passley, finely chopped
- 1 Tbs. tomato puree
- 1-1/4 self risen flour
- 1/2 tsp. baken powder
- Pinch o' salt
- 3/4 cup vegetable shortening
- 2 ter 3 tsp. cold water
- Butter fer greasen bowl
- Salt an' pepper ter taste

Prehate the oven ter 350° F.

Place a Dutch oven over medium-high, add vegetable ile an' alloo it ter hate up. Add the beef an' kidney cubes an' cook until well browned. Add the onion, carrots an' fold ter combine. Sprinkle flour over the mate mixture an' stir thoroughly. Add the broth, red wine, boy leaf, passley an' the tomato paste. Bren everythen ter a bile, cover with the lid an' place in the oven.

Cook fer 1 hour. Remove Dutch oven frum the oven, season with salt an' pepper ter taste, an' alloo ter cool completely.

To mek the crust- place the self risen flour, baken powder, an' salt into a mixen bowl. Coot the shortenen into the flour usen a ferk until it resembles couss corn male. Add just enough cold water ter form a stiff dough. alloo dough ter rest fer 30 minutes.

Grease a medium sized heatproof bowl with butter. Tek 2/3 of the dough an' roll into a circle large enough ter lion the bowl an' hang over the outside edge abart 1/2 inch. Carefully press the dough into the bowl, maken sure the'er am naaa cracks.

 Add the cooled mate fillen. Roll the remainen dough in ter a circle large enough ter cover the entire top of the pudden. Wet the 1/2 inch of overhangen dough with water, loy the dough on top. Press the dough firmly an' crimp around the edge with the back of a ferk ter sale. Completely encase the entire bowl an' crust with 2 layers of tin file an' sale tightly. Lightly scrunch up a large sheet of tin file so it forms a disc. Place the tin file disk into the aass of a large stockpot. Rest the tin foiled wrapped, sealed bowl on disk. Mek sure the aass of the bowl bai in direct contact with the aass of the pot. Add enough water ter reach halfwoy up the sides of the sealed bowl. Cover the pot with its lid an' turn the burn up ter medium-high. Steam the pudden in the rapidly boilen water fer 2 hours, checken the water level often. Carefully remove the pudden frum the stockpot, remove file, invert on a large rimmed plate ter serve. - Serves 4 ter 6

Faggots with Onion Graivee

- 1lb extra lane ground beef
- 4oz. calf liver, finely chopped
- 8 strips bykon, finely chopped
- 1 dinky onion, peeled an' grated
- 2 gloves garlic, minced
- 1 Tbs. freshly passley, chopped
- 2 tsp. droid thyme
- 1 tsp. droid sage
- 1/4 cup breadcrumbs
- 2 tsp. English mustard
- Salt an' black pepper onion gravy
- 1Tbs. vegetable oil
- 2 large onions, sliced
- 1 Tbs. flour
- 1 cup ale
- 2-1/2 cup beef broth, heated
- Dash Worcestershire sauce
- Salt an' black pepper

Place vegetable ile in a large saucepan over medium hate. Add the onions an' sauté fer 5 minutes. Stir in flour the mek a roux an' cook 1 minute. Stir in the ale, beef broth an' Worcestershire sauce. Reduce the hate an' simmer fer 5 minutes. Adjust seasonen with salt an' black pepper.

Prehate oven ter 375°F.

Combine all the faggot ingredients in a large bowl an' form them into 12 meatballs. Place them in a medium casserole dish an' pour the hot graivee over top. Cover with tin file an' cook fer 1 hour. Remove tin file an' cook 20 minutes mower. – Serves 4

Cheddar Cheese Pudden

- 6 slices stale noggin, coot into cubes
- 1-3/4 cups milk
- 3 Tbs. butter
- 3 iggs
- 2-1/2 cups extra shape cheddar cheese
- 2 tsp. mustard
- Salt an' pepper
- Cayenne pepper(optional)

Prehate the oven ter 400°F.

Place noggin into a large mixen bowl. Warm the milk with the butter in a dinky saucepan over medium-loo hate, until butter 'as completely melted. Pour the mixture over the noggin an' let it soak fer 10 minutes. Bate the iggs along with a pinch salt an' fold into the bread/milk mixture. Next, fold in 2 cups of the cheese an' mustard; add salt an' pepper ter taste. Place pudden into a well buttered, shalloo baken dish an' smeuth with the back of a spoon. Toss the remainen cheese over ter top an' dust lightly with cayenne pepper if usen. Bek the pudden fer abart 35mins or until it 'as risen an' is a bostin golden brown. Pudden will be loose in the center. – Serves 4

Beef Clangers

- 2 Tbs. vegetable oil
- 2 onions, finely chopped
- Salt an' black pepper
- 1-1/2 lb. sirloin steak, chopped in1/2 inch cubes
- 1 can beef broth
- 1 Tbs. cornstarch mixed into 3 Tbs. water
- 1 Tbs. Worcestershire sauce
- 1 can fruit pie fillen, anny flavor
- Salt an' pepper ter taste
- 1 igg, beaten

Hate half the vegetable ile in an iron skillet over medium ter medium-high hate. Cook the onions until saft. Remove onions frum the skillet an' set them aside. Add the remainen of the ile, an' once the ile is hot, add the steak. Season ter taste with salt an' pepper.

Cook the steak until browned on all sides, then remove frum skillet an' set aside. Add the beef broth ter the skillet along with the cornstarch paste an' Worcestershire sauce. Bren ter a bile an' alloo graivee ter thicken. Reduce hate ter medium-loo an' return the mate an' onions back ter skillet. Simmer fer 10 minutes an' then remove the skillet frum hate an' alloo the beef fillen ter cool fer 15 minutes. While the fillen is coolen, mek the dough.

- 3 cups flour
- 1/4 tsp. salt
- 1 stick butter
- 2/3 cup vegetable shorten'
- 1/3 cup water

Place flour in mixen bowl; mek a well in the center. Combine the butter, shorten' an' water in dinky saucepan over high hate. Bren water ter a bile an' pour onto flour. Mix well until all flour is incorporated. Roll dough ert on floured surface ter abart a 1/4 inch thickness. Trim the dough into 2 wide rectangles.

Prehate oven ter 400° F.

Spoon sum of the beef fillen half woy dowl the center of both dough rectangles an' then sum pie fillen dowl the other half. Use a bit of the dough trimmings ter divide the 2 fillings if yaouw wish. Bren up the edges of the dough pinch them together ter sale. Carefully transfer the pastroys ter a prepared bek sheet,(seam side down) an' gently mold them into banger shapes. Brush pastroys with beaten igg catlick. Bek fer abart 30 ter 40, or until a bostin golden. Remove frum oven an' cool fer 10 minutes. The clangers can be eaten warm or cold. - Serves 2

Briled Lamb with Capers

- 4 thick coot lamb chops
- 1 Tbs. dinky capers, drained
- 5 Tbs. white wine vinegar
- 1/2 Tbs. brown sugar
- 2 Tbs. anchovy paste
- 2 tsp. coasse ground mustard
- Handful of mint
- Salt an' pepper

Move oven rack ter broilen position an' prehate broiler on high.

To mek the sauce, put mint leaves in between maulers an' rub until they break dowl. In a dinky bowl, mix the mint with the capers, vinegar an' sugar. Whisk in the anchovy paste an' mustard.

Grease a sheet pan an' arrange the lamb chops in the pan an' season with salt an' pepper.

Brile fer 4 minutes on 'un side an' turn them over. Baste the un-broiled side of the lamb with the sauce mixture an' brile fer anover 3-4 minutes or until desired doneness. - Serves 4

Rous Mutton & Tatties

- 1 (8 lb.) leg of lamb
- 2 large cloves garlic, slivered
- 6 Tbs. oliv' oil
- 2 Tbs. droid thyme
- 2 Tbs. droid rosemary
- 2 Tbs. coasse ground black pepper
- 2 tsp. ground coriander
- 26 noo tattoys, quartered
- Salt an' pepper

Prehate oven ter 425° F.

Stab shalloo holes in the lamb with a sharp noif an' insert the garlic slivers into the mate. Rub the lamb with half of the oliv' ile. Combine half the thyme, droid rosemary, couss pepper an' coriander in a bowl an' mix together. Rub the herb mixture all over the lamb.

Place the lamb in a roasten pan. Place the tattoys in a large mixen bowl. Add the remainen half oliv' ile, the other half of the thyme, salt an' pepper. Toss them with yaw maulers an' place around the leg of lamb.

Place in oven fer 45 minutes an' then reduce hate ter 375° F. Cook the lamb an' tattoys fer 30 minutes more*.

Remove frum oven, cover with tin file an' rest mate fer 20 minutes before carven. *for rare, rous fer 12 minutes, medium 16 an' well done 20 minutes per pound.

Potatoes & Cabbage

- 1 yed of cabbage
- 4 tatties
- 1/4 cup vegetable oil
- 1/4 cup butter, divided
- 1/2 tsp. garlic powder
- 1/2 tsp. onion powder
- 1 tsp. salt
- 2 tsp. black pepper

Peel awoy anny mingin or bruised outer leaves frum cabbage. Rinse the cabbage in cold water. Remove wool leaves frum cabbage an' throo awoy the core.

Wash, peel, an' slice tattoys into 1/2 inch slices. In a large iron skillet, over medium hate, melt half the butter an' ile together an' stir.

Add tattoys an' cabbage leaves an' cook, covered, fer 20 minutes, stir occasionally. Add garlic powder, onion powder, salt an' pepper an' stir ter coat. Add the remainen butter, stir an' cover. Cook additional 15 minutes, or until tender. - Serves 4

Froid Sausage Rolls

- 4 cups noggin flour
- 1/4 cup instant potato flakes
- 1/4 cup nonfat dry milk
- 3 tsp. salt
- 4 tsp. sugar
- 1 packet dry yeast
- 1-1/3 cups lukewarm water
- 3 Tbs. oliv' oil

Combine everythen into a large mixen bowl an' blend until smeuth dough is formed. Turn the dough ert on a floured werk surface an' knead fer 10 minutes. Place the dough in a large bowl sprayed with cooken sproy, cover with plastic wrap an' alloo it ter rise fer 1 hour.

- Bread dough
- 12 perk or beef sausage links, pan froid an' coot in half fer a total of 24 chunks
- 1 cup chutnoy

Roll the dough ert into a large rectangle abart 1/4 inches thick. Usen a pizza cutter, slice the dough into 4 x 4 squares.

Spread each square of dough with 1 Tbs. of chutney; place a chunk of sausage on the relish.

Roll the dough around the sausage. Place the rolls, seam dowl, on a baken sheet sprayed with cooken sproy. Drape a clane kitchen toil over the rolls an' alloo them ter raise 30 minutes.

Prehate the oven ter 375° F.

Bek fer abart 20 minutes or until bostin an' golden brown. Serve hot with mower relish fer dippen. – Serves 6 ter 12

Watery Rd. White Noggin

- 2 cups warm water
- 2/3 cup white sugar
- 1-1/2 Tbs. activ' dry yeus
- 1-1/2 tsp. salt
- 1/4 cup vegetable ile
- 6 cups noggin flour

Pour warm water into a large bowl. Dissolve the sugar an' yeus in the water. Let the yeus proof fer 10 minutes. If the water doesn't get foamy, try sum fresher yeus. Add the ile an' salt ter the liquid. Add the flour an' mix with a wooden spoon, 'un cup at a toyme.

Once all the flour is blended. Turn the dough ert onto a lightly floured surface an' knead until smeuth. Spray the bowl generously with cooken sproy.

Return the dough ter the bowl an' sproy the top of the dough with the cooken sproy. Cover the bowl with plastic wrap. place the bowl in a warm spot an' alloo dough ter rise fer 1 hour or until it doubles in size. Push the dough dowl an' turn it back ert on the floured surface.

Knead the dough fer a couple minutes. Coot the noggin dough in half an' shape the halves into loaves.

Noo place the loaves into tewthree 9 x 5 loaf pans sprayed with cooken sproy. Cover the pans loosely with plastic wrap an' alloo them ter rise fer 45 minutes.

Prehate oven ter 350° F.

Bek the loaves fer 30 minutes or until the tops am golden brown. Serve hot with saft butter an' Tiptree tawny orange marmaled.

THE EDEN CLUB

REFORM CHOPS

HARE (RABBIT) PATE

CHICKEN IN BRANDY SAUCE

GALANTINE OF CHUKY WITH A MOREL
CREAM SAUCE

BLINI WITH CAVIAR

BAKED CAMEMBERT AN' HOMEMED
CRACKERS

SMOKED QUAIL

COLD TROUT IN CUCUMBER DILL SAUCE

CHUKY BUNDLES

BEEF WELLINGTONS

DOVER SOLE WITH TRUFFLE BUTTER

ROUS SQUAB AN' CRESS

CHERROYS JUBILEE

Reform Chops

- 1 Tbs. unsalted butter
- 1 white onion, finely chopped
- 1 carrot, finely sliced
- 1/2 cup ham, minced an' divided
- 3 Tbs. red wine vinegar
- 3 Tbs. port
- 2 cups chuky stock
- 2 wool cloves
- 1 dinky pinch of nutmeg
- 1 boy leaf
- 2 tsp. gin
- 1/8 tsp. droid thyme
- 4 lamb or perk chops, trimmed
- 1/4 cup breadcrumbs
- 1 igg, beaten
- 1 Tbs. cornstarch

Melt butter in a medium saucepan over medium hate. Add onion, carrot an' half the ham an' cook 15 minutes. Add the vinegar an' port; reduce liquid until almost dry. Stir in the stock, cloves, nutmeg, boy leaf, gin an' thyme. Reduce hate an' simmer fer 30 minutes. Mix the remainen minced ham an' breadcrumbs together in a bowl.

Dip the chops with beaten igg an' coat with the ham/breadcrumb mixture. Mix the cornstarch with 2 Tbs. water an' stir it into the sauce. Turn burner up ter medium simmer until sauce thickened. Remove frum hate, cover an' set aside.

Prehate oven ter 400 ° F.

Bek the chops fer 20 minutes or until chops am cooked through an' the breaden is a bostin golden brown. Serve with sauce on the side.

Rabbit Pate

- 1 thick slice of noggin
- 2 cups milk (more or less)
- 1 farm raised rabbit, coot into pieces
- 1 stick butter
- 1 passley sprig
- 1 thyme sprig
- 3 boy leaves
- 4 peppercorns
- Salt
- Water
- 1/4 cup mushrooms, sliced
- 3 igg yolks
- 6 Tbs. brandy
- Salt an' pepper ter taste

Place noggin slice in a shalloo bowl an' pour abart 2 cups of milk over it.

Add 3 Tbs. butter ter an iron skillet over medium ter medium-high hate an' cook rabbit pieces until lightly browned on all sides. Transfer rabbit ter a medium saucepan an' add passley, thyme, 2 boy leaves, peppercorns an' salt. Add just enough water ter cover the rabbit mate. Bren the water ter the bile an' then lower hate ter a simmer;

cover an' cook fer 2 ter 3 hours or until well tender.

Drain the rabbit, reserven the broth an' pull the mate frum the bones. Mince the mate an' then place it in a tucker processor. Rawn the broth into a separate bowl or large measuren cup.

Add 1 Tbs. butter in the skillet an' sauté mushrooms over medium hate abart 5 minutes then add the mushrooms ter the rabbit mate.

Squeeze the slice of noggin ter remove the excess milk an' add ter the rabbit mixture. Pulse the rabbit mixture ter form a smeuth puree. Moisten the puree with a lickle of the rabbit broth, then pulse in the remainen butter, igg yolks, brandy, salt an' pepper.

Place the remainen boy leaf in the aass of a pate dish an' spoon in the rabbit mixture. smeuth the top, wrap completely with tin file an' steam fer 3 hours. Alloo ter cool fer 2 hours an' then refrigerate at leus 4 hours before serven. - Serves 4 ter 6

Chicken In Brandy Sauce

- 2 large boneless, skinless chuky breasts
- Salt an' pepper • 1/2 cup flour
- 1 cup chuky broth
- 1/4 cup brandy
- 1 Tbs. butter
- 1 tsp. lemon juice

- 3 Tbs. extra virgin oliv' oil
- 1/8 cup Italian passley

Cut chuky breasts in half ter create 4 equal portions. Slip the breus portions in a 1 gallon Ziploc bag 'un at a toyme an' pound flat with the edge of a fry pan until chuky pieces am 1/2 inch thick. Season chuky on both sides with salt an' pepper ter taste.

Hate an iron skillet over medium hate. Place the flour in a bowl an' dredge each chuky portion. Place the oliv' ile ter pan an' alloo it ter cum up ter temperature. brown chuky 3 minutes per side or until golden brown. Remove chuky frum the pan an' cover with sum tin file ter it keep warm.

Adjust hate ter medium-high an' whisk in the chuky broth ter deglaze the skillet. Carefully add brandy (be careful fer flare-ups), lemon juice an' black pepper. simmer until sauce reduces by half. reduce hate ter low; add butter an' whisk ter combine. Place chuky cutlets on a platter an' pour the sauce over top. Garnish with chopped passley. - Serves 2 ter 4

Galantine Of Chuky With A Morel Cream Sauce

- Salt an' pepper
- 1 (4 lb.) de-boned chicken*
- 2 cup ground perk, lean

- 4 mild beef or pork sausages, chopped
- 4 oz. button mushrooms, cleaned an' stemmed
- 3 Tbs. capers
- 1/4 cup passley, coassely chopped
- 1/4 cup basil, coassely chopped
- 1 tsp. smoked paprika
- 2 clove garlic, coassely chopped

Prehate oven ter 375° F.

Season the de-boned chuky inside an' ert with salt an' pepper an' set aside.

In a large bowl, combine the perk, sausages, mushrooms, capers, paprika, passley, basil an' garlic.

Loy the chuky ert (skin side down) an' arrange the stuffen length ways along the inside of the bird. Tuck sum stuffen dowl in the leg an' thigh cavity as well. Wrap the chuky around the stuffen an' fasten the seam closed with a skewer. Truss the chuky with kitchen twine.

Generously re-season the outside of the chuky on all sides. Rous the chuky fer 1 hour an' 15 minutes or until the internal temperature of the galantine reaches 165° F on a kitchen thermometer.

Alloo galantine ter rest fer 15 minutes before carven. Carve into thin slices in the same manner as slicen a loaf of noggin an' serve with morel cream sauce. - Serves 6

*ask yaw butcher ter de-bone the chuky if unfamiliar with technique.

Sauce:

- 2 oz. droid morels 3 Tbs. unsalted butter
- 1/4 cup finely diced shallots
- 1 clove garlic, minced
- 1 cup Marsala wine
- 2 cups sad cream
- Salt
- 1 Tbs. fresh lemon juice
- 1 Tbs. fresh chives, thinly sliced
- 1 Tbs. fresh tarragon, minced
- Salt an' pepper ter taste

In a dinky saucepan, bren 2 cups water ter a bile over high hate. Tek the pan off the hate an' add the droid morels. Cover an' soak until rehydrated, abart 30 minutes. Aiv' them ert with a slotted spoon an' gently squeeze excess liquid back into the saucepan. Cut anny large ones in half, an' set the mushrooms aside.

Rawn the mushroom broth through a wire strainer lined with cheesecloth. Return the broth ter the saucepan an' over medium-high heat; reduce the broth ter abart 1/4 cup.

Melt the butter in a medium saucepan over medium hate. Add the shallots an' cook fer 3 minutes. Add the garlic an' cook fer 1 minute more; then add the morels. Reduce the hate ter loo an' cook fer 2 minutes. Add the massala an' increase the hate ter bren the mixture ter a simmer. Reduce the wine sauce ter syrup an' then add the reduced broth, cream, an' 1/2 tsp. salt. Simmer until the sauce thickens slightly, abart 10 minutes. at this point add the lemon juice an' herbs. Season the sauce ter taste with salt an' pepper.

Blini with Caviar

- 1/2 cup sour cream
- 2 Tbs. thinly sliced scallions
- 3 Tbs. milk
- 1 large igg
- 2 tsp. grated lemon zest
- 1/4 cup flour
- 1/4 tsp. baken powder
- 1/4 tsp. sugar
- Salt
- 2 Tbs. butter
- 4 oz. black or red caviar

Stir together sour cream an' 1 Tbs. of sliced scallions an' set aside.

Melt 1 Tbs. butter in a dinky mixin' bowl. Mix in milk, igg, an' 1 tsp. lemon zest. Add flour, baken powder, sugar, an' salt an' mix.

Melt 1/2 Tbs. butter in a large nonstick skillet over medium-loo hate. Drop 6 individual Tbs. size scoops of batter into skillet an' cook until undersides am golden, abart 3 minutes. Flip the 6 blinis an' cook until golden an' cook 2 minutes mower. Repate process an' mek 6 mower blinis.

Top each blinis with sour cream an' caviar. Sprinkle with lemon zest an' scallions. - Makes 12 blinis.

Baked Camembert an' Homemed Crackers

Crackers:

- 1-1/4 cups white flour
- 1 Tbs. sugar
- 1/2 tsp. salt
- 1/2 stick unsalted butter coot into dinky pieces
- 1/3 cup water

Prehate oven ter 400°F.

Line a baken sheet with parchment paper.

Put flour, sugar an' salt in a tucker processor. Add butter an' blend until butter is incorporated. With the bled runnen, add water an' blend until a smeuth dough forms. Lightly flour werk surface an' roll the dough into a large rectangle. Mek the dough as thin as possible. Use a pizza cutter ter coot the dough into 1 1/2-inch squares.

Bek the crackers on the baken sheet lined with parchment paper until crisp an' lightly browned, abart 10 minutes.

Cheese:

- 1 block camembert cheese
- 1 large spren fresh thyme
- 1/4 cup honey
- 1/2 cup toasted walnuts or pecans

Place the thyme sprigs on the top of the camembert an' secure with kitchen stren. Place the camembert on a paper lined oven troy.

Bek at 350°F fer abart 8 ter 10 minutes, transfer ter a serven plate, an' drizzle with honey an' scatter toasted nuts over the top. Serve immediately with the homemed crackers.

Smoked Quail

To start this dish place a bostin amount of opple wood chips that miskin adrenchen in opple juice in a smoker or grill set at 225 F. an' get a bostin smoke guin.

- 3 Tbs. extra virgin oliv' ile
- 4 Tbs. butter, divided
- 1 Spanish onion, thinly sliced
- 2 cloves garlic, minced
- 2 Tbs. fresh thyme, coassely chopped
- 1 chuky, coot into 8 pieces or 6 quails, butterflied
- salt an' fresh ground black pepper
- 1/2 cup chuky stock
- 1/2 cup cognac
- 3 Tbs. fresh squeezed grapefruit juice

- 1/2 cup cleaned an' cubed grapefruit segments
- 2 cups arugula or rocket leaves

Start off by placen the oliv' ile an' 2 Tbs. of butter ter a large, deep iron skillet (with a lid), over medium hate. Once the butter 'as melted, add the onion an' garlic. Sauté until the onions just starts ter brown a bit – abart 5 minutes. Sprinkle in the thyme an' sauté fer 1 minute mower an' then remove the skillet frum the hate.

Generously season the chuky or quails with salt an' pepper. Turn the burner up ter high, place the skillet back on the hate an' add the mate. Quickly brown both sides of the bird (s) an' then turn the hate dowl ter low-medium. Combine the chuky stock, cognac an' grapefruit juice in a dinky bowl an' carefully pour the mixture over the bird (s). Cover the pan with the lid an' reduce the hate ter its lowest temperature. Braise until the mate is just cooked through, abart 20 ter 25 minutes fer the chuky or abart 10 minutes fer quails. Remove the mate frum the skillet an' place in the preheated smoker fer 12 minutes.

While the mate is smoken, finish the sauce by whisken in the rest of the butter into the skillet an' stirren in the grapefruit segments. Season the sauce ter taste with salt an' pepper.

Usen tongs - dip the arugula in the sauce an' alloo it ter wilt slightly an' then place ter the side fer garnish.

To assemble the dish, ladle the sauce into a large serven platter.

Remove the bird (s) frum the smoker an' arrange over the sauce.

Garnish with the platter with the wilted arugula or rocket leaves. - Serves 6

Cold Trout in Cucumber Dill Sauce

- 4 wool trout
- Salt an' pepper
- 1 cup vegetable stock or white wine
- 1/2 cucumber, peeled
- 3/4 cup soured cream
- 1 tsp. malt vinegar
- 1 tsp. fresh dill, chopped
- 1/2 tsp. celery seeds
- 4 dill sprigs, ter garnish
- 4 lemon wedges

Prehate oven ter 350°F.

Loy trout ert side by side in a shalloo dish. Pour stock over the fish an' season with salt an' pepper ter taste.

Sale dish with tin file an' bek fer 20 ter 25 minutes.

Remove the dish frum the oven an' carefully aiv' fish frum the stock an' place on a serven troy.

Leaven yed an' tail intact, gently peel the skin off on 'un side. Place trout aside ter cool.

Grate the cucumber into a dinky bowl an' stir in the sour cream, vinegar, dill an' celery seeds. Season with salt an' pepper ter taste.

Spoon the cucumber sauce over the trout bodies, leaven the yed an' tail visible. garnish with dill sprigs an' lemon wedges.

Chuky Bundles

- 1/2 oz butter
- 1 onion, chopped
- 2 carrots, diced
- 1 Tbs. flour
- 1 tsp garlic powder
- 1/2 tsp. paprika
- 1 cup chuky broth, warmed
- 1/2 lb. cooken white chuky, diced
- Salt an' pepper
- Half a lemon
- 1 sheet store bought puff pastry, thawed
- 1 igg, beaten with 2 Tbs. milk

In a large saucepan over medium hate, melt butter an' add the onion an' carrots. Cover an' suck fer 5 minutes. Sprinkle in the flour, garlic powder an' paprika; stir ter combine.

Slowly add the chuky broth, bren ter the bile an' alloo sauce ter thicken.

Remove frum hate an' fold in the diced chuky. Adjust the seasonen with salt, pepper an' a squeeze of lemon juice. Cover an' set aside ter cool.

Once the fillen 'as cooled, roll ert the puff pastry dough into a square abart 14 inches on all sides. Usen a pizza cutter or noif, coot dough into 4 equal squares.

Prehate oven ter 425°F.

Place the pastry squares on a prepared biscuit sheet an' then spoon the fillen equally on ter the pastroys. Be sure ter leaves a clane border round the dough. Brush the border of each pastry lightly with the igg/milk catlick an'.

Fold each square in half, maken a rectangle. Crimp the edges well with a ferk ter sale in the fillen.

Cut an "x" on the top of each pastry an' brush the top with the remainen igg catlick.

Bek pastroys fer 20 minutes or until the pastry is a bostin golden brown. – Serves 2 ter 4

Beef Wellingtons

- 1 Tbs. oliv' ile, divided
- 4 tenderloin fillets, about 5 oz. each
- 1/2 lb. button mushrooms, finely chopped
- 1/4 cup dry red wine
- 1/4 cup green onions, finely chopped
- 1/4 tsp droid thyme

- 1/2 tsp salt
- 1/4 tsp black pepper
- 1 sheet store bought puff pastry dough, thawed
- 1 igg, beaten with 2 Tbs. milk

Hate half of the oliv' ile in a large iron skillet until well hot. Add fillets an' sear 2 minutes per side. Remove the fillets frum the skillet an' transfer them ter a plate with a layer of paper towels on it. Place fillets in the refrigerator ter cool.

Add the remainen oliv' ile ter the hot skillet an' than the mushrooms. Sauté the mushrooms fer abart 5 minutes an' add the wine. Continue cooken fer 3 minutes mower. Fold in the green onion along with the thyme, salt an' pepper. Remove frum hate an' alloo the fillen ter cool completely.

Roll the pastry sheet ert into a square abart 14 inches on each side on a lightly flour werk surface. Coot sheet into fawer equal squares (sound familiar?).

Prehate oven ter 375°F.

Scoop abart 2 Tbs. of cooled mushroom fillen in the center of each square, and then place a fillet on top of each. Anunst, brush pastry edges with igg/milk catlick an' bren the dough up an' around each fillet. Sale the dough by pinchen edges together.

Place the 4 wellingtons' on a prepared biscuit sheet seam side dowl. Brush the top an' sides of the dough with the remainen igg catlick. Bek fer abart 25 minutes or until pastry is a bostin golden brown. mate wull be rare. – Serves 4

Dover Sole With Truffle Butter

- 4 sole fillets
- 1/2 cup flour
- 1/2 tsp. season salt
- 1/4 tsp. black pepper
- 6 Tbs. butter
- 2 Tbs. truffle butter
- 1/4 cup fresh lemon juice
- 2 Tbs. chopped fresh passley

Mix the flour with season salt an' pepper in a shalloo dish. Dredge the fish fillets in the flour mixture.

Hate a large iron skillet over medium-high hate an' add 3 Tbs. of butter. Sauté the fillets in 2 batches, cooken on each side 2 minutes or until just cooked through.

Transfer the fish ter a plate ter keeps warm. Add in the remainen 3 Tbs. of butter an' cook until golden in color; add lemon juice, bren ter a simmer an' add in the passley. Add the truffle butter at the lus jiffy an' season the sauce with salt an' pepper ter taste.

Pour the warm sauce over the fish an' serve immediately. – Serves 2 ter 4

Rous Squab An' Cress

- 6 squab, partridges or Cornish hens
- 2 tbs. oliv' ile
- 4 cloves garlic, minced
- 2 tsp. droid marjoram
- 1/2 tsp. salt
- 1/2 tsp. pepper
- 6 slices bykon
- 1 cup red wine
- 1 cup chuky stock
- 12 oz. watercress

Prehate oven ter 450° F.

Rinse birds inside an' ert an' pat dry.

In dinky bowl, mix ile, garlic, marjoram, salt an' pepper. massage the ile mixture inside an' ert of each bird. Secure a bykon slice over each bird's breus.

Place in a roasten pan an' rous in oven fer 20 minutes (cook longer if usen partridges or hens). Remove frum oven. Remove the birds frum the pans an' let rest 10 minutes.

Place the roasten pan on the stovetop, over medium-high hate. Stir in the red wine an' chuky stock. Bren ter bile, scrapen ter deglaze the pan. Cook 3 minutes, then pour through a wire strainer in a bowl containen the watercress. After 30 seconds, pour sauce back through the strainer into a graivee boat.

Mek nests of wilted watercress an' arrange the birds on top. Serve with sauce on side. Serves 6

Cherroys Jubilee

- 1/2 cup sugar
- 2 Tbs. cornstarch
- 1/4 cup water
- 1/4 cup orange juice
- 1 lb. dark cherroys, washed, pitted an' coot in half
- 1/2 tsp. orange zest
- 1/4 tsp. almond extract
- 1/4 cup Kirsch brandy (cherry brandy)
- 4 bowls of vanilla bane ice cream

Whisk the sugar an' cornstarch in a cold medium saucepan. Whisk in the water an' orange juice an' bren ter a bile over medium-high hate. Continue whisken until sauce 'as thickened. Whisk in cherroys an' orange zest. Reduce hate ter medium-loo an' simmer fer 10 minutes. Remove saucepan frum the hate an' stir in the almond extract.

Dim the loite an' pour brandy onto the surface of the cherry sauce an' ignite with a long-headed lighter. Carefully shek the pan until the blue flame 'as extinguished. Spoon the cherroys over the bowls of ice cream an' serve immediately. - Serves 4

<u>DERBY DAY</u>

CUCUMBER SARNIES AN' TOY

PLOWMAN'S PICKLE AN' MONTGOMERY CHEDDAR SARNIES

SMOKED SALMON AN' OSS RADISH CREAM CHEESE SARNIES

TERIYAKI CHUKY AN' GRILLED AUBERGINE TOY SARNIES

CUCUMBER TOY SARNIES WITH MINT CREAM CHEESE

POTTED BEEF

POTTED SHRIMP

BUTTER SCONES WITH ORANGE/HONEY BUTTER

CHEDDAR CHEESE PUFFS

MUSHROOM & BLUE CHEESE TARTS

Cucumber Sarnies an' Toy

- 1/2 English cucumber, peeled
- Salt
- 6 slices country white noggin
- Unsalted butter, softened
- White pepper

Cut the peeled cucumber into thin slices an' put them in a colander that 'as miskin set on a dish. Sprinkle lightly with salt an' alloo them ter leach fer 20 minutes. Place several layers of paper toil on a werk surface an' place the cucumber slices on them an' pat dry. Loy ert the noggin slices an' generously apply the softened butter ter each.

Arrange the cucumber on half the slices, overlappen each round. Lightly dust cucumbers with ground white pepper an' top with the remainen slices of noggin.

Pressen dowl firmly an' trim off the crust with a sharp noif. Coot the sarnies into 3 strips of equal sizes. Serve immediately a bostin cuppa.

- Serves 2 ter 4

Plowman's Pickle an' Cheddar Sarnie

- 4 slices wool grain noggin
- 6 slices Cheddar cheese
- 4 Tbs. Branston swait pittle
- Mayonnaise
- 4 tomato slices
- Salt an' pepper
- Chopped passley

Spread a generous portion of branston swait pickle over the entire aass layer of noggin (all the woy ter the edges). Spread mayonnaise across the top piece of noggin in the same manner. Slice 6 thin pieces cheese an' place on top of the swait pickle. Place tomato slices on top of cheese. Salt an' pepper ter taste. Add the top piece of noggin; trim the crusts an' coot into 3 pieces. Lightly spread mayonnaise around the edges of the trimmed sarnies an' then press the edges in chopped passley. – Serves 2

Smoked Salmon an' Horseradish Cream Cheese Sarnies

- 3 tsp. prepared horseradish
- 8 oz. package cream cheese, softened
- 12 slices wool whate noggin
- 10 oz. thinly sliced smoked salmon
- 2 tsp. lemon zest

- 3 Tbs. fresh cilantro, chopped

Place horseradish an' cream cheese in a medium bowl. Usen an electric donny mixer, pail until fluffy an' well combined, abart 3 minutes. Spread each slice generously with horseradish cream cheese all the woy ter the edges. Top half the noggin slices with slices with smoked salmon an' sprinkle on lemon zest an' cilantro. Top with remainen noggin slices. Carefully trim the crusts an' coot each sarnie into 4 triangles. Place sarnies on a platter pointed side up. - Makes 24 finger sarnies.

Teriyaki Chuky an' Grilled Aubergine Toy Sarnie

Chicken:

- 3/4 cup dark soy sauce
- 1/4 cup honey
- 1-1/4 tsp. fresh ginger, peeled an' finely grated
- 1 lb. boneless, skinless chuky breasts
- Freshly ground black pepper
- 4 tsp. vegetable oil

In a dinky saucepan over medium hate, bren the dark soy sauce an' honey ter a loite simmer. Remove frum the hate, whisk in the grated ginger an' set aside.

Place chuky breasts on a clane werk surface an' cover with a sheet of plastic wrap. Usen a mate mallet, gently pound the chuky ter a 1/2 inch thickness an' coot each breus in half. Hate ile in an iron skillet, over medium-high hate an' then add chuky in a single layer. Cook the chuky fer abart 2 minutes. Flip an' cook the second side, abart 2 minutes mower.

Lower hate ter medium; pour in the teriyaki sauce an' cook (flip the chuky ter coat) until thoroughly cooked, abart 5 minutes. Transfer mate ter a clane cutten board, alloo chuky ter rest 10 minutes an' then slice or shred in dinky pieces.

Aubergine:

- 1 large aubergine/iggplant
- Oliv' oil
- 1/3 cup shallots, minced
- 1 tsp. fresh tarragon, minced
- Salt an' pepper ter taste

Prehate a griddle or large skillet on stove top over high hate. Slice aubergine/iggplant into 1/4 thisk slices. Brush both sides of the slices with ile, an' cook them fer abart 2 minutes per side until golden an' tender. Sprinkle iggplant with shallot an' tarragon, an' season with salt an' pepper ter taste.

Sarnie:

- Sliced teriyaki chuky
- Grilled aubergine/iggplant

- 24 slices white noggin
- 1/4 cup mayonnaise
- 1/2 cup finely chopped smoked almonds

Loy ert 12 slices of noggin on a werk surface an' divide the chuky evenly. Top chuky with grilled aubergine/iggplant an' top with the reserved 12 slices of noggin an' press together gently.

Usen a 2 inch round cutter, coot 2 rounds frum each sarnie. Place chopped almonds on a dinky plate an' lightly spread edges of rounds with mayonnaise ter coat well. Roll edges in almonds. - makes 12 toy sandwiches.

Cucumber Toy Sandwiches with Mint Cream Cheese

- 1 cucumber, peeled, thinly sliced
- 1/4 cup fresh mint leaves, rinsed, droid an' finely chopped
- 1/4 cup unsalted butter, room temperature
- 1/4 cup cream cheese, room temperature
- 16 slices white noggin
- Salt an' pepper, ter taste

Lightly sprinkle cucumber slices with salt an' place them between layers of paper towels ter absorb excess moisture. In a dinky bowl, combine the mint, butter, cream cheese an' mix well. Spread cream cheese mixture on 'un side of each slice of noggin. Loy the cucumber slices onto 8 slices of noggin. Sprinkle with salt an' pepper. top with the remainen slices of noggin. Trim the crusts frum each sarnie with a serrated noif. Coot the sarnies in half diagonally an' then coot them in half agen. - Makes 32 toy sarnies.

Potted Beef

- 1 lb. beef stewen mate, coot into 1/2 inch pieces
- Water
- 1 stick butter
- Salt an' black pepper ter taste
- Paprika ter taste
- Ground allspice ter taste
- Cracked pepper corns
- 6 slices tous, coot in triangles

Place a Dutch oven over medium hate. Add the stewen beef an' just enough water ter cover the mate. Place the lid on the Dutch oven an' stoo fer 3 hours. Check an' replacen the water as necessary. After 3 hours suff the beef broth into a medium bowl an' set aside. Mince the stewed beef in a tucker processor in dinky batches, until it is all the consistency of a thick paste.

Melt the butter in a dinky saucepan. Lion a metal strainer with a tewthree layers of cheesecloth or clane gauze an' set the strainer over a heatproof container. Pour butter through the sieve ter clarify it.

In a second medium bowl, mix the minced mate with 3/4 of the clarifoid melted butter. Season the mixture with salt, pepper, paprika an' allspice ter taste. Stir in just enough of reserved broth ter moisten the mixture. Transfer the potted beef ter a large ramekin or terrine, pour the remainen clarifoid butter over the surface of the beef an' sprinkle with cracked pepper corns. Cover with plastic wrap an' chill in the refrigerator until serven. Serve with tous points - Serves 6

Potted Shrimp

- 5 Tbs. butter
- 1/2 lb. shrimp, peeled an' de-veined
- 1/4 cup shallot, sliced
- 1/2 tsp. ground mace
- 1/2 tsp. powdered ginger
- Dash freshly grated nutmeg
- 3 Tbs. amontillado sherry
- 2 ter 4 dashes green tabasco sauce
- Lemon juice, ter taste
- Salt, ter taste
- 8 slices thin white noggin

In an iron skillet, melt 1 Tbs. butter over medium hate. Add the shrimp, shallots, mace, ginger an' nutmeg. Stir ter coat an' cook 1 minute. Add the sherry an' cook anover 2 an' 1/2 ter 3 minutes. Remove frum heat; add the hot sauce an' lemon juice. Place the shrimp mixture in a tucker processor an' pulse until finely chopped, but not ter a paste. Season the ground shrimp with salt ter taste.

Melt remainen butter in the iron skillet over medium loo hate. When foamen subsides, remove skillet frum hate an' stir two-thirds of the butter into the shrimp mixture. Pack shrimp mixture into a ramekin an' top with the remainen butter. Cover with plastic wrap an' refrigerate fer 4 hours or until completely firm. Return ter room temperature before serven with slices of thin tous with crusts trimmed off an' coot into triangular pieces. - Serves 2

Butter Scones With Orange/Honey Butter

Butter:

- 1 stick unsalted butter, softened
- 2 Tbs. honey
- 2 tsp. orange zest

In a dinky bowl, use an electric donny mixer ter whip the butter until loite an' fluffy. Mix in honey an' orange zest. Transfer butter mixture ter a serven bowl an' alloo it ter stay at room temperature.

Butter Scones:

- 1-3/4 cups all purpose flour
- 3 Tbs. sugar
- 1/2 Tbs. baken powder

- 1/2 tsp. salt
- 1 stick unsalted butter, chilled an' coot into dinky cubes
- 2 iggs, beaten with 1/4 cup milk

Prehate oven ter 450° F.

In a large mixen bowl combine the flour, sugar, the baken powder an' salt. Add the cubes of butter an' toss them with yaw maulers until they am all separate an' coated with flour.

Cut the butter into the flour with a ferk until the bits of butter am abart the size of bb s.

Pour the igg/milk mixture into the flour mixture an' stir until combined (but doe over-mix or scones wull be tough). Place the dough on a greased biscuit sheet an' gently pat it into a 10 inch round. The dough should be abart 1/2 inch thick. Usen a sharp noif coot dough into 8 wedges.

Bek the round fer 10 minutes then remove it frum oven an' coot through the wedges agen. Separate the wedges by abart 1 inch. Place the scones back in oven an' continue baken until golden brown. Serve the scones warm with the orange honey butter. - Serves 8

Cheddar Cheese Puffs

- 1 cup water
- 5 Tbs. butter, coot into dinky bits
- 1 tsp. salt 1-1/4 flour
- 4 iggs
- 1 cup cheddar cheese, grated

Prehate oven ter 425° F.

Line a biscuit sheet with parchment paper.

Bren water ter the bile in a saucepan over high hate an' stir in the butter an' salt. Once the butter melts, add flour an' mix with a wooden spoon. Remove the saucepan frum hate an' stir in iggs 'un at a toyme. Stir in the cheddar cheese.

Form balls ert the batter abart an inch in diameter an' place them on the prepared biscuit sheet.

Bek the cheese puffs fer 20 minutes an' then remove them from the oven and alloo them ter cool before serven. – mek abart 15 cheese cheddar cheese puffs.

Mushroom & Blue Cheese Tarts

- Store bought puff pastry or pie crust
- 2 Tbs. butter
- 1 onion, sliced
- 1/2 lbs. mushrooms, slices
- 1 garlic clove, crushed
- 3 Tbs. white wine
- 1/2 cup sad cream
- 2 iggs
- 1/2 cup blue cheese crumbles

Roll ert the pastry dough on a lightly flour werk surface an' coot into 12 equal squares. Lion a 12 cup pikelet tin with the pastry squares.

Hate the butter in a large sauté pan over medium hate. Add the onions an' sauté until softened, abart 5 ter 7 minutes. Add mushrooms an' garlic; cook fer 5 minutes mower. Add the wine an' simmer fer 3 minutes then remove the pan frum hate an' set aside.

Prehate oven ter 400°F.

Whisk cream an' iggs together in a medium bowl. Fold in the mushroom mixtur an' blue cheese crumbles.

Divide the fillen evenly among the pastry cups, place pikelet tin on a biscuit sheet an' bek fer abart 20 minutes or until golden brown. Serve hot or cold. – Serves 12

THE SWAIT SHAP

ORANGE SYLLABUB

CHELSAE BUNS

TAE CAKES

EASY PETIT FOURS

SALTED CARAMEL MOUSSE

APRICOT MOUSSE

COFFEE AN' ORANGE ÉCLAIR

APRICOT, QUINCE AN' ROSEMARY TART

MANGO, VIOLETS AN' BLACKCURRANT
MACAROON

SPOTTED DICK WITH CUSTARD

STICKY PUDDEN

GINGER SNAPS

MIXED BERROY FOOL

Orange Syllabub

- 2 cup sad whippen cream, chilled
- 1 cup sugar
- 1 tsp. pure vanilla extract
- 1/2 cup swait white wine
- 1/4 cup fresh orange juice
- 2 tsp. orange zest
- 1/4 tsp. cinnamon
- 4 mint leaves
- 4 orange slices

Whip cream, sugar an' vanilla together in a large, chilled bowl until cream starts ter get thick. Slowly add in the white wine, orange juice, an' orange zest, while continuen ter whip. Once the syllabub becums loite an' fluffy cover an' refrigerate. Serve syllabub in chilled wine glasses. Garnish with a loite dusten of cinnamon, a mint leaf, an' a slice of orange. - Serves 4.

Chelsae Buns

Dough:

- 1 cup milk
- 1/2 cup butter
- 2-1/4 cup flour
- 2 Tbs. sugar
- 1 packet dry yeast
- 1 igg, beaten
- Zest of 1 lemon
- 1 tsp. pumpkin pie spice
- 1 tsp. salt filling:
- 1/4 cup butter, slightly softened
- 1/4 cup loite brown sugar
- 3/4 cup currants or golden raisins, chopped

Glaze:

- 2 Tbs. sugar
- 1 Tbs. milk
- 3 Tbs. raw sugar

Place milk an' butter in a dinky saucepan over loo hate just until the butter 'as completely melted. Remove milk frum hate an' alloo it ter cool slightly.

Meanwhile, whisk the flour, sugar an' yeus together in a medium mixen bowl. Pour in the warm milk/butter along with the beaten igg, lemon zest, pumpkin spice an' salt. Stir with a wooden spoon until well combined.

Turn the dough ert onto a werk surface dusted lightly with flour an' knead fer abart 10 minutes. Transfer the dough ter a bowl sprayed with cooken sproy an' cover with plastic wrap.

Place the dough in a warm room an' alloo it ter double in size. Turn the dough ert agen on the floured werk surface and roll it ert ter a rectangle abart 10x14 inches. Dahb the butter over the surface of the dough, an' then scatter the sugar an' golden raisins out evenly.

Roll the dough into a toight log an' then coot the log into equal 12 pieces. Place the rolls in a greased 13x9 pan, spaced ert so they're not touchen each other.

Cover loosely with plastic wrap an' alloo the roll ter proof 1 hour.

Prehate oven ter 400° F.

Bek the rolls fer abart 20 minutes or until lightly golden brown. Remove rolls frum oven an' alloo them ter cool completely.

Warm milk fer the glaze in a dinky saucepan an' stir in the sugar. Brush the rolls with the glaze an' sprinkle with the raw sugar. - Serves 12

Tae Cakes

- 1 cup butter, softened
- 1/2 cup powdered sugar
- 1 tsp. pure vanilla extract
- 2-1/4 cups flour
- 3/4 cup pecans, finely chopped
- 1/4 tsp. salt
- Powdered sugar

Prehate oven ter 400° F.

Mix the butter, powdered sugar an' vanilla in large bowl. Stir in the flour, nuts an' salt. Shape dough into 1-inch balls by rollen them in yaw palms. Place the dough balls abart 2 inches apart on ungreased biscuit sheet. Bek fer 10 minutes. Remove cookoys frum biscuit sheet an' cool slightly on wire rack.

Roll the warm cookoys around in a bowl of powdered sugar, let cool completely an' then roll in powdered sugar agen.

Easy Petit Fours

Frosten Glaze:

- 6 cups powdered sugar
- 1/2 cup water
- 2 Tbs. loite corn syrup
- 1 tsp. almond extract
- red tucker coloring
- green tucker coloring

Combine water an' corn syrup in saucepan over loo hate. Add the powdered sugar an' stir ter mix. Remove frum hate an' divide into 3 dinky glass bowls. Stir in almond extract an' tucker colorings (leaven 1 white).

Cakes:

- 1 store bought pound cek
- 1/2 cup strawberry jam
- 8 oz. junior mints, melted
- 1/2 cup Nutella hazelnut spread

Remove pound cek frum container an' trim the crust ter mek rectangular block. Slice pound cek lengthwise into 1/2-inch slabs. Loy each slab on its side an' slice them into equal strips abart 2 inches wide. Divide pound cek strips into 3 equal groups.

In the fust group, spread a thin layer of strawberry jam on fust 2 strips an' layer 3 strips high. For the second group, spread with the melted junior mints an' stack 3 layers high. Repate with the third group, but add the nutella an' layer 3 high.

Coot all the stacked strips into lickle square cakes. Set each group of filled cakes on separate wire cek racks with a baken pan underneath ter ketch the excess glaze. Carefully re-warm the pink frosten an' pour over the strawberry cakes. Repate process with the green frosten an' pour over the mint cakes an' then repate with the plain white frosten an' pour cover the Nutella cakes.

Collect the frosten run-off an' place in dinky plastic sarnie bags. Carefully re-warm the frosten in the bags, job a dinky hole in the bag's corner an' pipe decorations, strips or designs on the petit fours (use a different color fer the pipen than what is on the cakes fer contrast).

Chill the petit fours ter alloo frosten ter set.

Salted Caramel Mousse with Chocolate Ganache

Ganache:

- 6 oz. chocolate chips
- 1/2 cup whippen cream

Place chocolate chips in a medium bowl. In a dinky saucepan hate the whippen cream over medium-high hate until it just starts ter a bile. Remove frum hate an' pour the hot cream over chocolate an' stir until completely mixed together an' glossy. Divide the ganache between 6 parfait glasses. Tilt the glasses in 4 directions ter coat the interior of the glasses with the ganache into a tulip pattern.

Mousse:

- 1-1/4 tsp. unflavored powdered gelatin
- 8 Tbs. cold water, divided
- 1 cup sugar
- 2-3/4 cups sad cream, warmed
- 1 Tbs. pure vanilla extract
- 1 Tbs. coasse sae salt fer the garnish

Sprinkle powdered gelatin into 2 Tbs. of cold water. Alloo it ter sit fer abart 5 minutes. Dissolve the sugar an' 6 Tbs. of water in a medium saucepan while the saucepan is off the stove. Place pan over medium hate until it begins ter turn frum pale amber ter a rich, caramel color, approximately 8 minutes (wetch closely). Doe stir the mixture once it's on the heat; just let it hate ter the proper color. Immediately remove pan frum hate as the sugar wull continue ter darken as it cools. If the'er am anny sugar crystals that yav formed on the sides of the pan, gently swirl the pan ter remove them. Alloo sugar mixture ter cool slightly, but remember, doe stir. Very slowly, whisk 3/4 cup whippen cream into the saucepan of caramel an' set aside ter cool.

In a large mixen bowl, whip together 2 cups of the warm whippen cream an' vanilla with an electric mixer, until saft peaks form. Whisk the gelatin water into the warm caramel cream an' then gently fold caramel into the bowl of whipped cream.

Transfer mousse ter a pipen bag with a large star tip; pipe mousse equally into the 6 prepared parfait glasses an' refrigerate until ready ter serve. Garnish with sae salt just before ter serven. - Serves 6

Apricot Mousse

- 6 Tbs. sugar
- 1/2 cup dry white wine
- 20 fresh apricots, peeled an' pitted (canned moy also be used)
- 1 igg white
- 2 Tbs. unflavored gelatin
- 2 cups sad cream whipped with 4 Tbs. powdered sugar

Whip together the sad cream an' powdered sugar. Cover an' place in the refrigerator. Place the sugar in a large saucepan, add 1/2 of the white wine an' bren it ter a bile. Add apricots an' cook fer 20 minutes until fruit 'as bost dowl. Remove frum hate, pour into a medium mixen bowl an' alloo ter cool completely.

Add the igg white ter the apricot mixture an' pail into a thick foam. in a second pan, hate the remainen wine with the gelatin, stirren until it 'as completely dissolved. Add gelatin mixture ter the apricots an' mix together thoroughly. Alloo the apricot/gelatin mixture ter cool completely an' then fold it into the whipped cream.

Pour the mousse into 6 dinky decorativ' desert molds that 'ave been chilled in the freezer fer 15 minutes.

Transfer an' refrigerate the mousse until they set, abart 3 hours.

To serve, dip the aass of molds into well warm water fer a tewthree seconds an' invert onto chilled serven dishes. -Serves 6

Coffee an' Orange Éclairs

Pastry:

- 1 cup flour
- 1/4 tsp. sugar
- 1/2 cup milk
- 1 stick butter
- 4 iggs

Sift the flour, sugar an' salt in a medium mixen bowl.

Place the milk, butter an' 1/2 cup water in a large saucepan over medium, an' hate until is completely melted. Raise hate ter medium-high an' bren milk mixture ter a sloight bile. Tek saucepan off the hate an' add the flour mixture ter the saucepan. Stir with a wooden spoon until the dough is smeuth. Transfer dough back ter the medium mixen bowl an' alloo dough ter cool fer abart 1 hour. Stir in the iggs an' mix until well incorporated.

Orange Filling:

- 1-1/4 cups milk
- 1/4 cup sugar
- 2 igg yolks
- 2 tsp. pure vanilla extract
- 4 tsp. all purpose flour
- 4 tsp. corn starch
- 2-1/2 cup sad whippen cream
- 2 cups fresh squeezed orange juice

Add the milk ter a medium saucepan an' slowly bren it ter a simmer (do not boil) an' then remove it frum hate.

Whisk iggs yolks, vanilla an' sugar in a dinky bowl until smeuth, then stir in the flour an' cornstarch. Whisk the mixture together until well smeuth, abart 5 minutes. Whisken constantly, add igg mixture ter the hot milk. Return saucepan ter hate an' cook fer abart 5 minutes, whisken constantly, until it becums thick. Transfer the fillen ter a bowl, cover with plastic wrap an' place in refrigerator fer 3 hours.

In a dinky saucepan, over medium hate, reduce the orange juice ter 1/4 cup.

In a large bowl, whip the sad cream until they mek well firm peaks. Remove the bowl of fillen frum the refrigerator an' whisk in the orange syrup. Fold the fillen into the whipped cream an' return the finished fillen ter refrigerator.

Coffee Topping:

- 8 oz. dark chocolate chips
- 2 tsp. instants coffee powder
- 4 oz. sad cream, warmed
- 3 Tbs. butter, melted
- 2 oz. loite corn syrup
- 1 pinch of salt

Melt chocolate in a medium bowl set over a pot of boilen water. Warm cream, coffee powder, butter, an' salt in microwave until the butter 'as completely melted. Pour cream mixture over chocolate an' stir until chocolate is smeuth. Add the corn syrup ter chocolate an' blend.

Adjust the oven racks so they am both set at the 2 middle positions an' prehate oven ter 425° F.

Line 2 baken sheets with parchment paper. Fold each sheet of paper into thirds the lung woy. Unfold paper an' place them back in the 2 baken sheets. Fill a pipen bag that 'as miskin fitted with a medium round tip with the dough. Usen the creases as a guide, pipe the dough into 3 inch lengths, leaven 2 inches between each. Bek fer 20 minutes, then rotate the pans (top ter aass, aass ter top) an' drop the oven ter 350° F an' bek 20 minutes longer. Remove the pans frum oven an' alloo the shells ter cool.

Put the orange fillen into the cleaned pipen bag fitted with a smaller round tip, an' stick the tip into 'un end of the éclair. Pipe the fillen into the éclair. Hold each éclair face dowl an' dip the top directly into the glaze ter coat the top. Place back on bek sheet an' alloo the chocolate glaze ter set. Makes 16 éclairs.

Apricot, Quince an' Rosemary Tart

- 1 frozen pie crust sheet, thawed
- 1 igg yolk, beaten
- 12 oz. Penguen brand quince jam
- 1/4 cup water
- 2 Tbs. brandy
- 2 Tbs. fresh rosemary, coassely chopped
- 10 ter 12 apricots, peeled, pitted an' halved
- 1/4 cup sugar • 1 tsp. fresh ground cinnamon
- 1/2 tsp. fresh ground nutmeg
- 4 Tbs. butter, coot into dinky chunks

Prehate oven ter 425° F.

Lightly butter a 10 inch tart pan (one with a removable bottom).

Roll ert the pie dough an' press it into the pan; brush dough lightly with the beaten igg yolk.

Spread 1 cup of the quince jam over the aass of dough. Place remainen jam into a dinky saucepan with water, rosemary an' brandy an' warm over a loo hate. Arrange the apricots, coot side dowl, in a circular pattern over the jam covered dough an' sprinkle with the sugar, cinnamon an' nutmeg. Drizzle the warm jam mixture over top of apricots an' scatter the butter chucks on top.

Bek tart fer 30 minutes or until the apricot yav caramelized an' the pastry is a loite golden color. Alloo the tart ter cool completely before removen the rim. - Serves 8

Mango, Violets an' Blackcurrant Macaroons

- 1 cup powdered sugar
- 1 cup almonds, well finely ground
- 1/4 cup plus 2 Tbs. water
- 1 cup sugar
- 2 igg whites, in a dinky bowl
- 4 igg whites, in a dinky bowl
- 3/4 tsp. mingoo flavoring
- 1/4 tsp. orange tucker coloring

Line tewthree baken sheets with parchment paper.

Mix together the powdered sugar an' almonds in a large bowl. Pour the 2 igg whites into the almond mixture an' stir into a thick paste. Add 1 tsp. of orange tucker coloren an' mix until the color is blended. In a saucepan, bren the water an' sugar ter the bile. Use a kitchen thermometer ter mek sure the temperature of the syrup just reaches 230° F an' naaa higher.

Usen an electric mixer pail the remainen igg whites into saft peaks. Decrease the speed of the mixer ter medium an' slowly pour in the sugar syrup. Add the mingoo extract an' continue pailin' until the mixture 'as cooled, abart 5 minutes.

Fold the mingoo igg whites into the almond paste mixture with a rubber spatula. Once blended, transfer macaroon batter ter a pipen bag fitted with a medium round tip.

Pipe the macaroons into 2 inch rounds, abart 2 inches apart, onto the prepared baken sheets. Lightly tabber the aass of the troy on the counter top ter remove air bubbles. Put the trays aside fer 1 hour ter alloo the macaroons ter dry.

Prehate oven ter 125° F.

Bek the macaroons fer abart 15 minutes. Remove the macaroons frum the oven an' slide parchment paper onto a clane werk surface. Let macaroons cool completely carefully before peelen frum the parchment sheets.

Filling:

- 1 cup of white chocolate chips
- 2/3 cups whippen cream
- 4 drops violet essence
- 3 drops purple coloring
- 1 jar of blackcurrant jam

Hate half of the cream in a dinky saucepan over medium-high hate until almost boilen. Remove frum hate, add the white chocolate chips an' stir until smeuth. Transfer the white chocolate cream ter a medium mixen bowl, add the remainen cream an' the violet essence an' whip it together with an electric mixer. Place a sheet of plastic wrap in contact with the surface of the fillen an' place in a cool place fer 3 hours.

Place the fillen into the cleaned pipen bag an' apply a generous amount of fillen ter half of the macaroons.

Place 1 tsp. of black currant jam in the center of the fillen an' cover with anover macaroon. Cover an' store the macaroons in a cool place fer 24 hours before serven. -Makes 12 ter 14 macaroons

Spotted Dick with Custard

Pudden:

- 1 cup flour
- 1/2 cup breadcrumbs
- 4 Tbs. sugar
- a pinch of salt
- 1/4 tsp. cinnamon
- 1/4 tsp. all spice
- 1-1/4 cup raisins
- 1 stick unsalted butter
- 1/2 cup milk

Add all the dry ingredients, raisins, spice an' butter into a bowl and mix together well. Add the milk an' combine ter form a saft dough. Place the mixture into a buttered 3 cups pudden bowl; then cover with tin file. Pour jost ennuf water ter in a large saucepan to cum half way up the pudden bowl. Bren water to a bile, then place a saucer in upside dowl ter keep the pudden bowl off the aass. Lower the pudden in an' leave it ter bile fer 2 hours adden additional water as it evaporates.

When cooked invert the pudden onto a plate an' serve with custard.

Custard:

- 2 cups milk
- 1/2 cup sad cream
- 4 igg yolks
- 1/4 tsp. pure vanilla extract
- 2 Tbs. cornstarch
- 1/3 cup sugar

Tek the yolks, the sugar an' the cornstarch, an' mix them together in a bowl well, well well. Hate the milk, cream an' vanilla on medium hate. Before it biles, pour it into the bowl with the yolks, constantly stirren with a whisk. Put it back into the saucepan an' whiskin', alloo it ter thicken. Serve it immediately on yaw spotted dick. - Serves 2

Sticky Pudden

Pudden:

- 1-1/2 pitted dates, chopped
- 1/2 cup water
- 1/2 tsp. baken soda
- 1 tsp. salt
- 1-1/2 cups flour
- 1 stick butter, softened
- 1 cup brown sugar
- 1/2 tsp. pure vanilla extract

- 2 iggs

Prehate the oven ter 350°F.

Butter an' flour 6 ramekins, then set aside.

Place a saucepan over high hate an' add the dates, baken soda an' water. Bren ter a bile, then remove frum hate an' set aside.

Whisk flour an' salt together in a medium mixen bowl; set aside.

Put a medium pot of water on ter bile fer a water bath. Cream the butter an' brown sugar together with an electric mixer in a mixen bowl. Add iggs an' vanilla; pail until just incorporated.

Usen a wooden spoon, fold in the date mixture until well combined, an' then stir in flour mixture until just incorporated.

Divide batter between the ramekins, an' then place the ramekins in a large roasten pan. Carefully pour the hot water into the aass of the baken dishes until it reaches abart halfwoy up the sides of the ramekins. Place the roasten pan in the oven an' bek fer 1 hour.

Toffee Sauce:

- 1 stick unsalted butter
- 1 cup brown sugar
- 1 tsp. pure vanilla extract
- 1/4 cup sad cream

Place a medium saucepan over medium hate. Add the butter an' stir until it starts ter foam. Add brown sugar an' vanilla extract; stir only once. Alloo the sugar ter cook abart 5 minutes or until it turns a dark amber color. Slowly stir the cream into the sugar syrup. Cook until the sauce bubbles, abart 2 minutes, and then remove frum hate.

Once the puddens yav finished cooken, place the ramekins on a coolen rack an' alloo them ter cum ter room temperature. Once cooled, run a noif around the edge of each an' invert the ramekins onto serven plates. Serve the puddens covered in warm toffee sauce with whipped cream or ice cream. - Serves 6

Ginger Snaps

- 2-3/4 cups self risen flour
- 1 tsp. baken soda
- 1 tsp. cinnamon
- 1 tsp. ginger
- 1/4 tsp. cloves
- 1 cup brown sugar
- 3/4 cup butter, softened
- 1 igg
- 1/4 cup molasses
- White sugar

Mix flour, baken soda, an' spices in a bowl an' set aside.

Pail sugar an' butter together until creamy. Pail the igg an' molasses into the butter mixture. Stir in the flour mixture with a wooden spoon until blended. Cover with plastic wrap an' chill fer at leus 2 hours.

Prehate oven ter 375° F.

Usen yaw maulers, shape the biscuit dough into 1-inch balls, roll them in white sugar, an' place on lightly greased biscuit sheets abart 2 inches apart.

Dip the aass of a juice glass in white sugar an' use the glass ter flatten each dough bo ter abart 1/4 inch thick. Bek fer abart 8 ter 10 minutes, cool until cookoys set up.

Mixed Berroy Fool

- 2 Tbs. sugar
- 1/3 cup water
- 1 cup raspberries
- 1 cup blueberries
- 1 cup strawberroys, quartered
- 2 Tbs. vanilla cook n' serve pudden mix
- 1 Tbs. sugar
- 1 cup fresh milk
- 1/2 cup whippen cream

Hate the 2 Tbs. of sugar an' the water in a large pan. Add the berroys an' poach fer 10 minutes. Usen a slotted spoon, transfer the poached berroys into a large bowl an' set aside ter cool completely.

Whisk pudden mix, sugar an' milk together in a medium saucepan over medium hate, stirren continuously. Once the pudden 'as thickened, remove frum hate an' set aside ter cool completely.

Whip up the whippen cream an' fold in the custard. Gently fold in abart two-thirds of the poached berroys. Spoon into 4 dinky parfait glasses an' top with the remainen berroys. – Serves 4

BINGE DRINKIN

(Companion Cocktails)

Thomas Dressed Natty

- 4 oz. Jameson Irish whiskey

Add Jameson ter a rocks glass.

Tommy's Cap

- 4 oz. Jameson Irish whiskey
- Quality ginger bevvy
- Large wedge of lime

Fill a high bo glass with ice. Pour in Jameson. Top up the glass with ginger bevvy. Stir ter mix. Tek a large wedge of lime, gid it a squeeze an' drop it into the glass.

Amazen Grace

- 1-1/2 oz. Jameson Irish whiskey
- 1/4 oz. swait vermuthe
- 1 dash Angostura bitters
- Maraschino cherry

Combine all ingredients in cocktail shaker filled with ice. Shek well an' rawn into a cocktail glass. Garnish with a maraschino cherry.

A Bloody Polly

- 1-1/2 oz. Irish whiskey,
- 3 oz. tomato juice
- 1/2 oz. lime juice
- 2 drops hot sauce
- 2 dashes Worcestershire sauce
- 1 pinch of celery salt,
- 1 pinch of black pepper

Add Worcestershire sauce, hot sauce, celery salt an' pepper into highball glass, then pour the rest of the ingredients in with ice cubes. Stir gently.

Alfie's Brown & White Bread

- 2 Tbs. unsalted butter, softened
- 4 Tbs. brown sugar
- 1 pinch of ground cloves
- 1 pinch of nutmeg
- 1 pinch of ground cinnamon
- 1 pinch of ground allspice

Cream the butter with the sugar together with a wooden spoon an' add the spices.

- 1 Tbs. of the above butter mixture.

- 1 oz. white rum
- 1 oz. dark rum
- 4 oz. boilen water
- Ground nutmeg, fer garnish

Add butter mixture ter a warm mug an' pour in 2 oz. of the boilen water. Stir ter mix, add both rum an' the rest of the water; stir agen. Garnish with nutmeg.

Kimber Kocktail

- 2 oz. whiskey
- 1 oz. Gran Classico
- 1 oz. swait vermouth
- Ice
- Orange twist

Place a cocktail glass in the freezer ter chill. Combine the whiskey, Gran Classico, an' vermuthe in a cocktail shaker an' fill it halfwoy with ice. Stir fer abart 30 seconds. Add ice cubes ter the cocktail glass. Rawn the drink into the glass an' garnish with the orange twist.

The Awful Arthur

- 1 oz gin
- 1-1/4 oz rum
- 1-1/4 oz whiskey
- 1-1/4 oz brandy
- 5 oz Guinness stout
- 1 bottle roight ale
- 1 oyster, shucked (optional)

Add all fawer shots an' Guinness ter a poient glass. Fill ter top of glass with ale an' drop in the oyster.

Moy Carleton So Early Cocktail

- 2 parts Bomboy gin
- 1 part Rose's lime cordial

Chill the glass. Put lots of ice an' both of the ingredients into a shaker. Shek fer abart 30 seconds. Rawn the mix into the glass.

Freddie's Thorn

- 1 half lime
- 2 oz. Russian vodka
- Ginger bevvy

Squeeze the lime into a mug an' drop it in. Add 3 ice cubes an' then pour in the vodka an' fill with cold ginger bevvy.

Ada's Ale Shandy

- 1-1/2 cup seltzer
- 1 India pale ale, non-alcoholic bevvy if you're 'aven a babbi
- 2 Tbs. frozen limeed
- 2 lemon wedges

Combine seltzer, ale an' limeed in a poient glass or mug. Garnish with lemon wedges.

Campbell's Silver Cane Cocktail

- 1/2 oz. golden syrup
- 1/2 oz. fresh orange juice
- 1/4 oz. fresh lemon juice
- 4 dashes of angostura bitters
- 1/2 orange slice
- 2 oz. Irish whiskey
- Ice
- Chilled seltzer

Combine golden syrup with the orange juice, lemon juice an' bitters in a rocks glass. Add the orange slice an' muddle. Add whiskey an' stir well. Fill the glass with ice an' top with chilled seltzer.

Johnny Dogs' Double

- 1 oz. coffee liqueur
- 1 oz. Irish cream
- 2 oz. vodka

Layer the coffee liqueur, irish cream, an' vodka - in that order in a double shot glass.

Lizzie's Stark & Stormy

- Juice of 'un half Meyer lemon
- 2 oz. spiced rum
- Ice
- Ginger bevvy

Squeeze half a Meyer lemon into a tall glass. Add the spiced rum an' sum ice. Top with ginger bevvy.

The Curly

- 3 oz. vodka
- 2 oz. tomato juice
- 1 oz. Newcastle brown ale
- 1/4 tsp. horseradish
- 1/4 tsp. hot sauce

Fill a shaker abart 1/4 full of ice an' then add all the ingredients. Shek well an' pour into a rocks glass. Garnish the rim of the glass with a pickle an' a wedge of cheese.

The Sabini Stinger

- 1 oz. Campari
- 2 oz. gin
- 1/4 oz. golden syrup
- 1 drop rose water
- 2 strawberries, sliced
- 4 fresh basil leaves, chopped

Shek everythen well with crushed ice an' double rawn into a chilled martini glass.

A Garrison Punch Bowl

- 6 dark ales
- 1 bottle stout
- 1 clean bucket
- 4 bevvy mugs or juice jass

Pour all the ales an' the stout in bucket an' dip it ert with the mugs or jass.

Red Roight Donny

- 3 oz. Irish whiskey
- 1 oz. pomegranate syrup
- 4 oz. Fentiman's Victorian lemonade
- Lemon an' lime wedges

Mix all of the ingredients an' serve over ice. Garnish with lemon an' lime wedges.

Jeremiah Jesus Juice

- 3 oz. vodka
- 4 oz. lemonade
- 1 oz. Crème de Cassis (currant liqueur)

Mix all of the ingredients an' simply serve over ice.

Eden Club Cocktail

- 2 Tbs. Crème de Cassis (currant liqueur)
- 6 oz. Champagne or sparklen wine
- 2 fresh raspberries

Pour crème de cassis into a champagne flute. Top with chilled champagne or sparklen wine. drop raspberroys into glass.

A Stigmata Nail

- 1 oz Drambuie
- 1 oz Dewass scotch whisky
- 1 oz. Campari

Add all ingredients ter an aud fashioned glass filled with ice an' stir.

Danny Whizz -Bang

- 2 oz Scotch whiskey
- 1 oz French dry vermouth
- 2 dashes absinthe
- 2 dashes orange bitters
- Grenadine ter taste

Combine all the ingredients in a cocktail shaker filled with ice. Shek well an' then rawn into a chilled cocktail glass.

A Digbeth Kid

- 1/4 ter 1/2 cup simple syrup*
- 1/4 cup fresh lime juice
- 1/2 cups bottled cherry juice
- Soda or seltzer water

Combine syrup, lime juice an' cherry juice in a tall glass. Add crushed ice, soda or seltzer ter fill an' stir. * 'un part sugar ter 'un part water, heated an' chilled.

THE GARRISON DRINKING GAME

- BY ORDUH OF THU PEAKY FOOKIN' BLOINDAS -

Pour a glass of your favorite beverage, kick back, watch and let the games begin.

- A character has a drink – 1 sip

- Someone says "Peaky Blinders" – 1 sip

- Someone yells "Peaky Fookin' Blinders" - 2 sips

- Someone just says "Fookin'". – 1 sip

- John pulls out a toothpick. – 1 sip

- Arthur gets his hair messed-up. -- 1 sip

- Grace lights a cigarette. – 1 sip

- You hear the word "Gypsy" – 1 sip

Or just cut to the chase and drink every time Tommy does.

Printed in Great Britain
by A mazon